HISTORY THROUGH
MATERIAL CULTURE

MANCHESTER
1824

Manchester University Press

IHR RESEARCH GUIDES

General editor: Lawrence Goldman
Series editors: Jonathan Blaney, Simon Trafford and Jane Winters

This series is for new researchers in history. By offering a practical introduction to a sub-discipline of history, each book equips its readers to navigate a new field of interest. Every volume provides a survey of the historiography and current research in the subject; describes relevant methodological issues; looks at available primary sources in different media and formats and the problems of their access and interpretation. Each volume includes practical case studies and examples to guide your research, and handy tips on how to avoid some of the pitfalls which may lie in wait for the inexperienced researcher.

The guides are suitable for advanced final-year undergraduates, master's and first-year PhD students, as well as for independent researchers who wish to take their work to a more advanced stage.

Already published
Using film as a source   Sian Barber

HISTORY THROUGH MATERIAL CULTURE

LEONIE HANNAN AND SARAH LONGAIR

Manchester University Press

Published by Manchester University Press
Altrincham Street, Manchester M1 7JA

www.manchesteruniversitypress.co.uk

British Library Cataloguing-in-Publication Data
A catalogue record for this book is available from the British Library

Library of Congress Cataloging-in-Publication Data applied for

ISBN   978 1 7849 9126 5   paperback

First published 2017

Typeset in ITC New Baskerville Std by
Servis Filmsetting Ltd, Stockport, Cheshire
Printed in Great Britain by
CPI Group (UK) Ltd, Croydon CR0 4YY

CONTENTS

List of illustrations   vii
Acknowledgements   ix
Glossary   xi

Introduction   1
1 Approaches to the material world   15
2 Planning a research project   43
3 Developing a methodology   70
4 Locating sources: understanding museum collections and
   other repositories   95
5 Analysing sources   121
6 Writing up findings   141
Afterword   159

Select bibliography and resources   163
Index   178

ILLUSTRATIONS

0.1	Rowntree's 'Dairy Box' tin.	*page* 2
1.1	Woodcut of the *Wunderkammer* room, from the book *Dell'historia naturale* by Ferrante Imperato (Naples: C.Vitale, 1599).	16
2.1	Diagram illustrating range of questions that can be asked of an object, and subsequent avenues to pursue.	47
2.2	Benjamin West, *Joseph Banks* (1773).	50
2.3	Andrea Mantegna, *Adoration of the Magi* (c. 1495–1505).	54
2.4	Olowe of Ise, Palace of the Ogoga of Ikere (c. 1900).	60
2.5	Loving cup with two handles, with portrait of Horatio Nelson, flanked by trophies with inscriptions including the phrase 'England expects every man to do his duty' and a verse praising Nelson (c. 1820).	63
3.1	A sketch by Vivienne Richmond of a pair of hand-stitched drawers found in the English Girls' Friendly Society Archive.	81
4.1	(a and b) Chinese spoon (top and underside) found on the East African coast, showing the accession number marked on the underside.	101
5.1	Object analysis protocols.	124
5.2	(a and b) Object records. Sketch of earthenware pot by Joey O'Gorman.	126
5.3	Pair of chopines (c. 1550–1650).	135
5.4	Pair of chopines (c. 1600).	136
5.5	Pair of chopines (c. 1590–1610).	136
6.1	(a, b and c) Sample object label format and two examples.	150

ACKNOWLEDGEMENTS

Over many years, we have both been fortunate to work with a great number of colleagues, students and visitors in museums, galleries, universities and collections whose insights have informed our understanding of the material world and have therefore been fundamental to the writing of this book. We would like to express our deep gratitude to all of these inspiring people, who are too numerous to name individually. During this period of work, we have been particularly indebted to colleagues and friends at UCL Museums & Collections, Queen's University Belfast, the British Museum and the University of Lincoln for their support.

While we have been compiling this guide, several people have generously given up their valuable time to advise on aspects of the text or to discuss particular issues. Our thanks go to Katy Barrett, Laura Basell, James Davey, Mark Gardiner, Lydia Hamlett, JD Hill, Deborah Howard, Bryony Millan, Claire Reed and Rebecca Wade. Vivienne Richmond also kindly gave her permission for us to reproduce her sketch of a pair of hand-stitched, prize-winning drawers, for which we are most grateful.

Working with our editor Emma Brennan and the team at Manchester University Press has been a very positive experience and they have made the challenging task of writing such a book both enjoyable and rewarding. The series editors at the Institute of Historical Research and the anonymous readers have provided invaluable, astute and constructive advice, which has helped enormously towards making a growing and dynamic field such as material culture history accessible for our readers.

We first came to know one another when we participated in the 100 Hours project, funded by UCL's Centre for Humanities Interdisciplinary Research Projects in 2013. This experiment in material culture research (the brainchild of Leonie and of Kate Smith, now at the University of Birmingham) brought together ten researchers to work on ten objects, for 100 hours. Together, we encountered an intriguing array of objects, approaches and people, and the participants have become valued colleagues and friends, who have all influenced the text of this book in different ways. This experience also laid the foundations for our own working partnership. The 100 Hours project would not have been possible without the particular support and enthusiasm of the late Professor Lisa Jardine. We hope that she would be pleased with this book both as an outcome of our collective study of objects and as a method of supporting future students in making the study of the material world central to their historical practice.

Belfast and London, June 2016.

GLOSSARY

This glossary explains terms used within and relevant to this book, giving accepted dictionary definitions (*Oxford English Dictionary*) or focusing upon their usage in material culture scholarship as appropriate. Words in italic refer to terms defined elsewhere in the glossary.

accession	the formal legal process of recording a new item into an existing collection of books, paintings or *artefacts*.
accession number	the series of letters or numbers identifying an object in a collection, also referred to as a *registration number*.
acquisition	the administrative, decision-making and *documentation* process involved in adding an object to a collection.
agency	the capacity of something or someone to act and effect change in its environment.
antiquarian	relating to the study of antiquities.
antiquary	a person who studies or collects antiquities, also sometimes referred to as 'an antiquarian'.
Antiquity	the period of the ancient past that commences with the *classical* period and ends before the Middle Ages. As a common noun, it refers to the ancient quality of something: 'an object of great antiquity'.
artefact	an object made by a human being, typically one of cultural or historical interest.
bespoke	made to measure or to order.
capitalism	an economic and political system in which trade and industry are owned privately and run to make a profit.
cast	an object made by using a mould, sometimes referring to a replica of an existing *artefact*.

classical   relating to ancient Greek or Latin literature, art, architecture or culture.

classification   the act of categorising things into different groups.

classmark   a series of numbers or letters that forms part of a *classification* scheme to identify individual objects within a collection.

colonialism   the process of acquiring partial or full control over another country or territory, sometimes involving settlement, and exploiting it economically.

commodity   a material thing that can be bought and sold, that holds value and that can be exchanged.

connoisseur   an expert judge, usually in matters of art and culture.

connoisseurship   the practice of being an expert judge in matters of taste. Connoisseurship within art history scholarship refers to the practice of identifying artworks of individual artists through close analysis of the work and in-depth knowledge of their technique and wider body of work.

conservation   the act of conserving; prevention of injury, decay, waste or loss. In contrast to *restoration*, conservation emphasises arresting deterioration over repairing an object to look as it once did. 'Preventive conservation' is the practice of creating the optimum conditions for an object's storage/transport and so on to prevent deterioration or damage. 'Interventive conservation' refers to practice of a conservation taking a form of action directly upon an object, such as cleaning and repair.

context   the circumstances that form the setting for an action or an idea, which are important for their understanding.

conversation piece   a genre of painting in which the people appear in a social group in a landscape or (often) a domestic setting; a popular genre in the eighteenth century.

custodian   a person or organisation which has the responsibility to look after and protect a given person, thing or collection of things.

documentation   (in museums and other *repositories*) official records relating to items in a collection, including (but not limited to) identification details and descriptions;

provenance; associations with people, places and dates; condition; treatment; and present location.

early modern this term refers primarily to European history and refers to the period between the end of the 'Middle Ages' and the beginning of the 'Industrial Revolution', or from the late fifteenth to the late eighteenth centuries.

empirical describing evidence, data or conclusions derived from observation, experiment or investigation, rather than theoretical analysis.

engraving a print made from an engraved plate, block or other surface, or the process or art of engraving a design on a hard surface, especially to make a print.

ephemera things which were created to have a temporary or transient existence, intended by their makers originally to be discarded, such as posters and tickets.

ethnography the systematic study and description of peoples, societies and cultures.

excavation (in archaeology) process of exposing, processing and recording archaeological remains, at an excavation site.

genealogy line of descent traced through a person's ancestors; the word also refers to the study of and tracing of lines of descent.

Georgian of or characteristic of the reigns of the British Kings George I–IV (1714–1830).

guild confraternity, brotherhood or association formed for the mutual protection of its members, or for undertaking some common purpose. It is often applied to such organisations in the *medieval* and *early modern* periods in Europe, and such groups often had a particular 'guild-hall' as their meeting place.

high relief a method of moulding, carving, or stamping in which the design stands out from the surface, to a greater (high relief) or lesser (low relief) extent.

historiography the study of the writing of history and of written histories.

iconography (art history) the identification, description, *classification* and interpretation of symbols, themes and subject matter in the visual arts.

interpretivism (social sciences) the belief that research into the social world requires different tools from those applied in analysing the natural world, in contrast to *positivism* and *empiricism.*

inventory detailed list of the property (include items and land) of a person at the time of their death, often describing the item and its value.

materiality the material or physical aspect of a thing; the quality of being composed of physical matter.

medieval (in European history) relating to the period between the ancient and *modern* eras, approximately from AD 600 to 1500.

methodology a method or body of methods used in a particular field of study, a description of which often includes justification of the suitability of the techniques used in it.

mezzotint a print made from an *engraved* copper or steel plate, the surface of which has been scraped and polished to give areas of shade and light respectively. The technique was much used from the seventeenth to early nineteenth centuries for the reproduction of paintings.

microscopy use of a microscope.

modern refers to the period of history after the French Revolution and the 'Industrial Revolution' or the nineteenth, twentieth and twenty-first centuries.

patina thin coating upon a surface, usually the result of weathering or burial.

patronage (art history) action of a patron in commissioning a work/works of art, or, more broadly, using money and/or influence to advance the interests of an artist or style.

photogrammetry technique of using photographs to ascertain measurements, for example in surveying and mapping.

plastazote a type of foam often used for protective storage and packaging for objects as it is stable and non-reactive with most other materials.

porcelain impermeable ceramic material made from china clay also known as kaolin, often used for making vessels and other objects.

positivism a philosophical system underpinned by an *empirical* understanding of science, and that philosophical propositions can be scientifically tested and proven or falsified. It also refers to those who believe that one of the principal roles of philosophy is to analyse the language of such propositions.

proletarian relating to the proletariat or so-called working class.

provenance the place of origin or earliest known history of something or a record of ownership of a work of art or an antique, used as a guide to authenticity or quality.

qualitative adjective describing the assessment of the quality of something.

quantitative adjective describing the measurement or assessment of the quantity of something.

reception the way in which people react to someone or something.

registration number the series of letters or numbers identifying an object in a collection, otherwise referred to as an *accession number*.

Renaissance refers either to the revival of European art and literature under the influence of *classical* models in the fourteenth to the sixteenth centuries, or more generally to this period of European history when there was a new interest in science and ancient art and literature, especially in Italy.

repository a place in which things may be deposited or stored, often now used in reference to institutions such as museums, galleries and libraries devoted to the storage and protection of historical books and objects.

restitution the act of returning something to its previous owner, particularly relevant in the case of material in museums taken or acquired through force or questionable means.

restoration the action of returning something to a former owner, place or condition. In contrast to *conservation* it implies repairing an object to look as it did originally.

Romantic of or characteristic of the literary, artistic, musical and intellectual movement during the late eighteenth and nineteenth centuries in Europe, which had an emphasis on feeling, individuality and passion rather than *classical* form and order.

sculpture   a) the act of creating a form in two or three dimensions by building up (e.g. with clay) or removing material (e.g. carving in wood or marble), or *casting*; b) as a noun, the form created using these techniques: a sculpture.

spectrometer   a scientific instrument or apparatus used for recording and measuring a spectrum, which can aid the analysis, for example, of the types of material from which an object is formed.

spoliation   the act of despoiling, pillaging or plundering; seizure of goods or property by violent means.

structuralism   in cultural and social anthropology, any theory or mode of analysis which deals with the structure or form of human society and social relationships.

symbolic   (art history) describing use of symbols or set thereof, which associate meanings to particular people, objects or places.

Victorian   of or characteristic of the era in British history during the reign of Queen Victoria, from her accession to the throne on 20 June 1837 until her death on 22 January 1901.

INTRODUCTION

As long as humans have made material things, material things have shaped human history. They were the things people in the past sat on, wore, ate from, hunted with, treasured, wrote upon, wrote with, traded, exchanged and longed after. Material things influence our needs and define our aspirations; they express our ideas, encode value and convey messages (Figure 0.1). For historians, finding ways to access the values and meanings embodied within material things brings the past into clearer focus.

For many of us, it is the things of the past – whether encountered in the attic, in the museum or in the landscape – which first inspired our interest in history. This interest might be prompted by an aesthetic appreciation of an object, an emotional engagement with its owner or simply a memory of that moment of discovery and the curiosity it prompted – what is it, why is it here and what does it mean? This is one form of engagement most of us can relate to when we consider the charm of a treasured artefact. As Sherry Turkle has put it, 'We think with the objects we love; we love the objects we think with.'[1] But then there are also the ordinary things, the overlooked, the everyday – they fill our worlds, make our routine actions possible (or obstruct them). We cannot – as Lorraine Daston has emphasised – even 'imagine a world without things'.[2] Material culture frames all of our actions and experiences and is constitutive of them. Material culture sheds light on our production and consumption of goods, our power relations, social bonds and networks, gender interactions, identities, cultural affiliations and beliefs. Material culture communicates all kinds of human values, from the economic or political to the social and cultural. And whilst historical objects cannot offer a direct and clear window on past worlds they are a powerful form of evidence, and a 'provocation to thought'[3] they are as complex, deceptive, partial and multi-layered as textual survivals.

0.1 A Rowntree's 'Dairy Box' tin (purchased 1953). This product containing assorted chocolates was launched by Rowntree's, a British chocolate business, in 1937. Confectionary was rationed during the Second World War, a regulation which remained in place until 1953. This box belonged to a former colonial officer, purchased en route to West Africa for his first posting shortly before the end of rationing on confectionary. He retained the box as a memento of his journey, in particular the memory of the ship's shop allowing him to buy as much as he wished as rationing did not apply there. This was shown to Sarah Longair in 2016 as part of a British Academy / Leverhulme Trust Small Research Grant project entitled 'Objects of Colonial Memory'. Author's photo.

Since the mid-1970s, disciplines across the arts, humanities and social sciences have experienced a real surge in interest in material culture, which is sometimes referred to as 'the material turn'.[4] This proliferation of work on the material world has inspired many historians, working across a wide range of subjects and periods of time. As a consequence, there is now substantial scholarship on the value of material objects for historical research, which often appears in the form of edited collections. Seizing the moment when historical material culture studies is now well established, this student-orientated research guide illuminates how we as historians can engage with material sources in practice. In the preceding paragraph we outlined how exciting and important material culture can be. In the chapters that follow, we will show how you can turn instinctive curiosity into rigorous historical research. What follows is, therefore, a practical introduction for students and researchers who wish to use objects and material culture as primary sources for the study of the past. Throughout this guide, you will find case studies that offer tangible examples of current historical work – their questions, methods and analyses – but it is intended to be read alongside published research on material culture. In the references and suggested reading (located at the end of each chapter) you will find avenues for further enquiry. Here, we use examples drawn from the early modern period through to the twenty-first century, from a wide range of geographical locations, and aim to challenge researchers to try new ways of working as well as providing the guidance necessary to do so. Histories of the last five centuries have been driven to a remarkable extent by textual records and it is with this in mind that *History through Material Culture* offers researchers a step-by-step guide to approaching the material evidence that survives from around 1500 to the present day.

Whilst many readers may be registered on an undergraduate or a postgraduate course at a university, this guide is written for anyone with an interest in history and material culture. We hope that the structure of the guide, taking you from planning through to writing up a research project, will be as useful to individuals working outside of academia as to those working within universities and colleges. Material culture research might just as easily be prompted by a visit to a museum, a new job or a conversation with a relative as it is by a formal course of study or assignment.

Anticipating that many researchers will feel under-skilled or lacking in confidence in tackling artefacts of the past, we will trace the process of research from the conception and development of the research questions through to the writing-up of findings – giving particular attention to the ways in which objects can be located, accessed and understood. This practical guidance is augmented by the use of examples of seminal and contemporary scholarship in this interdisciplinary field, so that readers can see how particular approaches to sources have been used to develop historical narratives and arguments. From the start of their historical studies, students can and should use objects and images not simply as illustrations but as key primary sources. However, the study of objects does require specific, yet acquirable and transferable, analytical skills which will enrich an interrogation of the past and provide avenues for original thought. To this end, *History through Material Culture* will de-mystify both the process of researching objects and the way research practice relates to published scholarship and, in doing so, enable researchers new to material culture to pursue their research questions to the full.

Of course, when we work with material culture – like any historical source – we are dealing with a partial historical record and must negotiate both the presence and absence of evidence and the reasons for them. Moreover, the vast majority of material things from the past have not survived to the present day. There are two main factors that determine survival: material composition and societal values. An object's materiality and how it has been treated have an important role in determining its physical survival. For example, stone and ceramic objects endure well in many environments, as do metals if they are not exposed to water. For this reason, ceramics and coins are some of the objects most commonly excavated by archaeologists and can provide vital clues to the date of a site. Meanwhile, textiles survive poorly in the ground and are prone to material disintegration more generally – whether from attacks by insects or through decomposition, to which all organic matter is at risk. Aside from material resilience, there are many social factors that have an influence on the survival of some objects over others. In the most basic sense, this relates to the way objects are valued by the society in which they were made and by subsequent societies. Everyday objects of low monetary value may be highly prevalent in a society of origin but be rare survivals over centuries because of their perceived insignificance. Meanwhile, objects that are highly expensive or rare at the time of their making might retain their value to society over time, ensuring their survival. These different perceptions of value (economic, cultural or social) have played an important role in collecting practices and, for objects, residing within a collection has a protective effect – making them more likely to remain intact. So, again, the factors that made some objects more likely to be collected and kept than others have had a hugely important influence on what we have access to today.

Objects matter / object matters

This is an exciting time to be incorporating material culture more explicitly within historical research. There has been a wealth of academic publications since the beginning of the twenty-first century which demonstrate the exciting potential of taking a material approach to historical themes and topics. We shall draw upon these throughout this book. Museums are increasingly opening up access to their collections offering abundant primary source material. The pioneering History of the World in 100 Objects project, a collaboration between the British Museum and the BBC, demonstrated how a single object could offer a view into a historical period. In these fifteen-minute radio programmes, the close examination of an individual object initiated an exploration of the many contexts in which the object could be understood, from its makers to the history of its arrival in the museum's collection. As a radio programme with downloadable podcasts, the project responded to contemporary methods by which the public engage with historical content. During each programme a range of commentators from different cultural backgrounds discussed the themes prompted by the object – far more than could be included in an object label in a museum setting. The series prompted listeners to examine the images online or visit the museum and listen to programmes in front of the objects themselves. The programmes inspired numerous projects and publications on the model of 'A History of X in X Objects'. Naturally, there are criticisms of the approach: in some cases the objects gained a greater prominence and iconic status through the programme than they actually enjoyed at the time of their making; in others the links from object to context were sometimes deemed to be tenuous. Nonetheless, A History of the World in 100 Objects has undoubtedly been hugely influential in moving an object-driven approach from the academic sphere firmly into the public realm.

THE ACADEMIC LANDSCAPE

There have always been good reasons for researchers to engage with material culture, and changes in universities since the mid-1990s have encouraged interest in this kind of work. In the United Kingdom and elsewhere, researchers have been asked to think more deeply about the impact of their research in wider society. Responses to these changes have varied, and academics have robustly defended the need for research that answers fundamental questions rather than meeting specific societal challenges. However, many researchers have been prompted to think about the opportunities that do exist to make their research meaningful beyond the university's walls. For historians in particular, museums and heritage organisations have proved especially important collaborators in the production and communication of research. Museums and heritage organisations have a dual role as the custodians of valuable architectural, object and archival collections and also as public institutions with a mission that includes engaging their diverse audiences of visitors. In periods of economic recession, museums and heritage sites have often found their budgets stagnate or reduce, placing pressure on activities that are considered non-essential. In these conditions, collaborations between researchers and heritage sites can prove particularly beneficial, combining complementary skills and knowledge to achieve shared aims. Put simply, where academics might be rich in the time and skills needed for primary research but poor in terms of their abilities to deliver societal impact, museums tend to maintain their broad public audiences but struggle to resource new research on their collections. A plethora of recent partnership projects have shown that, with a little bit of care and consideration of different working cultures, collaboration across these sectors is not only achievable but also rewarding.[5]

In this research guide we will be discussing a range of academic disciplines that have purchase on the study of material culture in all its different forms. These same disciplines, to a large extent, predict the ways in which object collections have been organised in institutions today. These disciplines include archaeology, social anthropology, art history, human geography, design and the decorative arts, literary studies and, of course, history itself. In Chapter 1 the different approaches to thinking about material culture that have emerged from these fields of study will be explored in detail. Throughout this guide, we will retain a focus on what researching material culture means for historians and how we can use these sources to answer key questions of historical enquiry. However, we will also recognise the ways in which using material culture can help the discipline of history to change, develop and ask new questions about the past.

For disciplines like history, a focus on material culture is inevitably compared with the more traditional source material – text. Historians have always relied on the written word to understand society in the past and are relatively unused to considering artefacts that do not contain words. Moreover, historians have traditionally viewed history as a political process and focused their energies on the study of the elites who held the reins of power in society. Taken together, this over-reliance on the textual record and emphasis on the elite, institutional, legal and political were mutually reinforcing, as the most powerful actors in society were the most likely to leave a formal record of their lives, lives that enacted political power over others. However, whilst the powerful were able to leave a record in words, we must also acknowledge that many (often most) people in the past were illiterate and where low-status individuals did leave texts behind, they rarely survive. Non-elite lives did not always revolve around text – and objects could be seen as a way of reaching the histories of the ordinary, the everyday, the non-elite and the non-literary. It would certainly seem sensible to use the wealth of material sources that survive from times past, as well as their textual equivalents. And most historians who use material culture as a source choose to combine it with other textual sources.

For researchers seeking new territory, museums and historic sites have much to offer. Even well-known collections in large, national museums such as the British Museum or the Science Museum in Manchester have not been heavily used by historians. Moreover, the large and the famous represent only a small proportion of the collections open to the public and available to researchers. Across the world there are small, independent museums, hidden, institutional collections, local town or county museums, specialist collections in historic houses, little-known house museums in urban areas and remote collections in rural locations. With a little bit of work and some general protocols in mind, it is possible to gain access to many of these collections and the historical worlds they can help open up. In Chapter 4, we will discuss in detail the different ways in which you can locate and access collections for research purposes depending on the kind of institution in which they are held.

TERMS AND DEFINITIONS

In the various literatures relating to the study of objects, there are many definitions of the term 'material culture' as it has become a defining and cross-disciplinary concept for research on the material world. As Susan Pearce comments, terms such as 'object', 'thing', 'specimen', 'artefact' or 'good' describe individual pieces or groups of things, whereas 'the term "material culture" [is] used as a collective noun'. She stresses that 'All of these terms share common ground in that they all refer to selected lumps of the physical world to which cultural value has been ascribed.'[6] In the 1970s, the anthropologist James Deetz qualified: 'Material culture … is not culture but its product. Culture is socially transmitted rules for behavior, ways of thinking about and doing things … Material culture is … that sector of our physical environment that we modify through culturally determined behavior.'[7] A decade later, the specialist in American studies Thomas Schlereth asked the question 'Who first fabricated the slightly awkward expression: "material culture"?' Schlereth traces its use back to the elaborately named anthropologist and collector Augustus Henry Lane-Fox Pitt-Rivers who, writing in 1875, encouraged his readers to 'consider material culture as the "outward signs and symbols of particular ideas of the mind."'[8] For Schlereth's purposes, then, material culture is usefully defined as 'that segment of humankind's biosocial environment which has been purposely shaped by people according to culturally dictated plans.'[9] This emphasis on contact with people and a relationship with human culture is common in literature on material culture studies. In fact, the term 'artefact' denotes the hand of humankind in the making of an object in contrast to things that are produced by nature alone. In museums, this distinction between the man-made and the natural is articulated by the terms 'artefact' and 'specimen'. As Linda Hurcombe has described:

> An artefact is defined as anything made or modified by people, so artefacts are not just 'things' but are intricately linked with people's needs, capabilities, and aspirations. All societies and the individuals within them use objects to define, punctuate, and manipulate their social personae.[10]

Amiria Henare comments, more simply: 'Artefacts may be broadly understood as material objects that are or have been in touch with people.'[11] Of course, this definition leaves open the possibility of natural specimens which have been appropriated by people for cultural reasons to be understood as 'artefacts'. Susan Pearce takes this view, arguing:

> I would contend that specimens from the natural world work within human society in exactly the same ways as human artefactual material, whatever they may do in nature and under only the eye of God. They are a part of the human construction of the world both as single pieces and (but rather more obviously) as collections.[12]

The term 'material culture' works well as it emphasises the idea that materiality is part of culture and proposes that the social world cannot, therefore, be fully understood without attending to its material realities. However, to date, historians working on material culture have tended to emphasise the 'culture' over the 'material'.[13] In Chapter 3 we will explore in detail examples of recent historical scholarship on material culture in order to illuminate the different ways in which researchers use material evidence or evidence of material culture to make historical arguments.

In this guide we will focus our discussion on three-dimensional, man-made objects which pertain to the study of a people or culture. However, as there are no clear boundaries for the historian between a ceramic vessel and a manuscript miscellany as potentially useful primary sources, we will also refer to objects such as paintings (as art works) and photograph albums (as archival, visual culture). Art works, in particular, occupy an important place within historical material culture studies. Aside from the status of paintings or prints as valuable historical sources, they are also present us with visual images of a huge variety of objects from the past. It is often by looking at a painting that we will first encounter an object of interest, whether that artefact is foregrounded in the piece (as in the case of still lives) or whether it augments the main subject of the painting.

If you are working with 'art works', one aspect of your enquiry relates to what makes them valued. Once again, context is critical. An object is only determined as a work of 'art' by the value and prestige attached to the skill of the creator and, therefore, the aesthetic value of the thing.[14] Art works are often characterised by a sense of their being one-off creations – unique, rare and costly to purchase. However, visual culture also indicates how societies choose to represent themselves in the present and in relation to the past. For example, in the Renaissance, the revival of interest in Antiquity and the classical era revolutionised philosophy, literature, art and architecture. Using visual material as supporting evidence can also be very helpful in answering questions concerning the value of material culture. For example, Dutch genre interiors of the seventeenth century depict in detail objects in domestic settings, which is very useful for learning more about their use, meaning and value. However, as with portraits or paintings of political events, these images must be critically assessed to disentangle issues of artist, genre, symbolism and representation.

Objects may also combine elements of the textual and the visual or have been created, at least in part, with concern for artistic presentation. Take, for example, a photograph album – combining as it does the photographs themselves; the annotated text that might accompany them; identifying places, individuals or dates; and also the material construction of the album itself as a bound book. An object of this kind demands analytical skills that can attend to its composite nature and the different challenges of decoding the individual images versus the album as a whole. Where an album might encompass a variety of media, other objects might prompt us to consider where their boundaries lie. For example, if we think of buildings as a category of material culture then should we look at the building alone – its bricks and mortar, its architectural design – or do we also need to consider the environment it occupies? What parameters should we draw for ourselves? This depends to a large extent on the questions we wish to answer, but there is a strong argument that the study of material culture – in its acknowledgement of the importance of materiality – requires us to attend also to the spaces occupied by material things. However, where rooms, buildings and landscapes all have material qualities to analyse, we might also think about the 'intangible heritage': living culture that resides in communities, practices and traditions (such as dance and music) and ways of remembering collective pasts.[15] This last category of heritage is outside of the scope of this guide, but can become pertinent to studies of material culture as they relate to a diverse range of cultural practices.

Research project: a common structure

1. Project summary (What is this about? What are the research questions and why are they interesting and important?)
2. Background (What has been written about this before and by whom?)
3. Methodology (What, if any, theoretical frameworks are you using? What approach will you take? What methods will you use?)
4. Sources (What will you use and why? Where are they located?)
5. Outcomes (What will be produced at the end of this research project?)

READING THIS GUIDE

This research guide is organised in such a way as to lead you through the different steps involved in preparing and carrying out a research project which uses material culture. The guide acknowledges that historical research takes many forms and that many studies may only use objects as one small part of their evidence base. Nevertheless, whilst acknowledging the diversity present in historical material culture studies today, we focus here on what needs to be done to develop a project that is strongly focused on material culture and which is likely to involve the direct study of artefacts in museum or heritage collections. With this in mind, the guide begins with a broad discussion of the approaches that can be taken to thinking about material culture and moves on to the practical steps required in planning research, formulating research questions, developing a methodology, locating and analysing sources, and, finally, writing up your findings. If you have a clear sense already of the direction you wish to take, this guide will act as a prompt to proceed methodically and to get the most out of your research. If, on the other hand, you are just beginning to think about studying objects, you will find within these pages a summary of the field in which you hope to work and a range of possible routes forward. This guide will work best if it is taken up at the beginning of planning a research project and referred to regularly – in this way, it will act as a research companion, raising questions and offering possible solutions at each stage. Writing a research proposal is often the first step in devising a project (see box) and being able to describe the aim of the project, position it within the existing literature and explain what evidence you will be analysing and why will be invaluable as you progress.

Chapter 1 will provide an introduction to the origins of historical material culture studies in terms of both academic research and museum practice. In particular, approaches developed in anthropology, archaeology and art history will be explored. The origins of the study of objects will also be traced through the history of collecting and collections, showing that objects take on alternative meanings as they move from the culture of their origin to the cabinets of museums. The theoretical underpinning of material culture studies will be elucidated and the discussion will demonstrate that by viewing the objects of the past as inanimate and inactive as compared with the living, breathing humans who made, exchanged and used them, researchers can miss the dynamism of the object–person interactions that took place many decades or centuries ago. Finally, the chapter will discuss the circumstances that brought about historical material culture studies. In particular, the realisation amongst historians of the 1960s and 1970s that for writing histories of indigenous peoples, slave communities or the poor and illiterate, textual records did not hold the answers. It concludes with a summary of the key trends in historical material culture research today.

In Chapter 2, we explore the strategies for incorporating material culture as a primary source and show how material culture research can be employed to make historical arguments. This chapter makes clear that there is significant variety in the ways in which scholars and practitioners look at material culture and that these differences are primarily driven by the fact that art historians, literary scholars, curators and cultural geographers ask different questions of material things. This chapter also shows how object-specific questions create important and vital studies in and of themselves, but also how they can contribute to overarching research questions with wider historical significance.

Chapter 3 shows that, very roughly, we can divide historical approaches to the study of material culture into two: the study of the object as the primary subject and the use of material culture to promote new perspectives on historical questions. The chapter uses a series of case studies of historical work that deploys material culture in different ways, focusing on the selection of primary sources, modes of analysis and the role of material culture in the project as a whole. Finally, this chapter discusses examples of scholarship that deal with the material but which lack relevant and accessible artefacts to research. This is a common difficulty for historians for whom collections do not adequately support their chosen subject. Dealing with the absence of things will become important for many historians working in this field, and this section will provide some practical tips for negotiating this challenge to the research process.

In Chapter 4, we focus on how you can find out where different kinds of material culture might be located in museums, galleries, historic sites or private collections. The chapter attends to the practical concerns of how to use object catalogues, communicate with curators and negotiate different kinds of institutions. Whilst the emphasis is placed on locating and accessing material culture that you can work with directly, digital resources in terms of online catalogues and image resources are also covered, as these can provide both a first step in discovering relevant material and also a helpful point of reference as your project develops.

Chapter 5 looks at the methods you can employ to analyse individual objects or collections as part of the research process. These include observation and careful recording of objects in text, sketch and diagram form and also forms of analysis that are reliant on equipment such as photography and microscopy.

Chapter 6 considers the different formats in which you might wish to present your work, from exhibition labels and blogposts to an essay or dissertation. This chapter addresses features of writing-up that are particular to the use of material culture.

A short afterword summarises the key points found within this research guide, and a bibliography and resources section at the end of the book provides opportunities for further reading and investigation. We hope that this guide will equip the student or researcher with the necessary tools to undertake material culture research in history and forge new ground in this exciting and expanding field.

NOTES

1 S. Turkle (ed.), *Evocative Objects: Things we think with* (Cambridge, MA: MIT Press, 2007), p. 5.
2 L. Daston (ed.), *Things that Talk: Object lessons from art and science* (New York: Zone Books, 2008), p. 7.
3 Ibid.
4 H. Green, 'Cultural History and the Material(s) Turn', *Cultural History*, 1:1 (2012), 61–82.
5 See, for example, the Share Academy Project; the Thames Valley Country House Partnership project; the National Alliance for Museums, Health and Wellbeing; and the Yorkshire Country House Partnership.
6 S. M. Pearce (ed.), *Interpreting Objects and Collections* (New York: Routledge, 1994), p. 9.
7 J. Deetz, *In Small Things Forgotten: The archaeology of early American life* (New York: Anchor Press, 1977), p. 35.
8 T. J. Schlereth, 'Material Culture Research and Historical Explanation', *The Public Historian*, 7:4 (1985), 21–36, p. 21.
9 Ibid., 22.
10 L. M. Hurcombe, *Archaeological Artefacts as Material Culture* (London: Routledge, 2008), p. 3.
11 A. J. M. Henare, *Museums, Anthropology and Imperial Exchange* (Cambridge: Cambridge University Press, 2005), p. 3.
12 Pearce, *Interpreting Objects*, p. 1.
13 F. Trentmann, 'Materiality in the Future of History: Things, practices and politics', *Journal of British Studies*, 48:2 (2009), 283–307.
14 This point was provocatively made by Marcel Duchamp with his exhibiting of a standard urinal in a gallery – transforming an everyday, mass-produced article into a work of art.
15 For more, see L. Smith and N. Akagawa (eds), *Intangible Heritage* (London: Routledge, 2009).

RECOMMENDED FURTHER READING

Auslander, Leora, 'Beyond Words', *American Historical Review*, 110:4 (2005), 1015–45.

Candlin, Fiona, and Raiford Guins (eds), *The Object Reader* (New York: Routledge, 2009).

Gerritsen, Anne, and Giorgio Riello (eds), *Writing Material Culture History* (London: Bloomsbury, 2015).

Greig, Hannah, Jane Hamlett and Leonie Hannan (eds), *Gender and Material Culture in Britain since 1600* (Basingstoke: Palgrave, 2015).

Harvey, Karen (ed.), *History and Material Culture: A student's guide to approaching alternative sources* (London: Routledge, 2009).

Hicks, Daniel, and Mary C. Beaudry (eds), *The Oxford Handbook of Material Culture Studies* (Oxford: Oxford University Press, 2010).

MacGregor, Neil, *A History of the World in 100 Objects* (London: Allen Lane, 2010).

Turkle, Sherry, *Evocative Objects: Things we think with* (Cambridge, MA: MIT Press, 2007).

Woodward, Ian, *Understanding Material Culture* (London: Sage, 2007).

✻ 1 ✻

APPROACHES TO THE
MATERIAL WORLD

There are, as we have seen, very many reasons for historians to be interested in the insights that material culture can unlock. However, for objects to yield rewards we must employ tried and tested strategies for examining them. Such established approaches have emerged from distinct disciplines and professional practices, which have their own histories and intellectual concerns. This chapter provides an introduction to the origins of historical material culture studies in terms of both academic research and museum practice, so that we can understand not only which approaches to the study of material culture are available to us, but also the reasons why these approaches were developed in the first place.

There are myriad ways in which objects can be investigated and these largely depend upon the research questions being asked or the stories objects are expected to communicate. Academic disciplines have approached material culture as evidence in different ways, and some disciplines – such as archaeology, anthropology and art history – have a long track record of engaging with material things and, therefore, an established legitimacy in their modes of analysis. Likewise, museums are environments which foster highly specialised working practices around objects, practices that are intended both to aid the long-term survival of artefacts and to engage, educate and inspire diverse public audiences.

By contrast, subjects such as history or literary studies, which have only incorporated the study of objects comparatively recently and in the context of disciplinary traditions that prioritise text, have looked to other disciplines and curatorial practice for inspiration. Frameworks and methodologies for working with objects as historical evidence have, therefore, been harvested from several quarters. As we shall see, some scholars use objects as a means of experimenting with their own research practice, whilst others seek to absorb the study of material culture into the over-arching demands of history as a discipline. Here, we will start with the philosophical basis for our understanding of material culture, before considering the ways in which archaeologists, anthropologists, art historians and curators (amongst others) have thought about 'things'. From this point we will trace the origins of historical material culture studies in the 1970s and the way that field has developed since. In each section we will focus on selected key works, but this is by no means an exhaustive treatment of the subject and we will point to further reading that might be helpful.

THE FOUNDATIONS

Commodities and gifts

Artefacts from bygone and contemporary times have long fascinated humans, who have consistently collected, treasured, traded and displayed

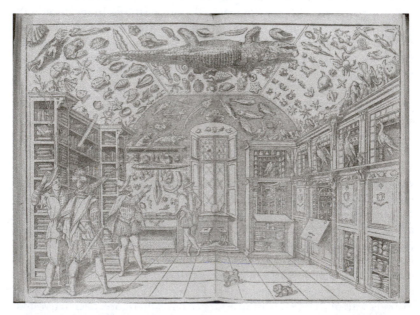

1.1 Woodcut of the *Wunderkammer* room, from the book *Dell'historia naturale* by Ferrante Imperato (Naples: C. Vitale, 1599). L0072645. Courtesy of the Wellcome Library, London, available under CC BY 4.0.

objects of special value. In the early modern period, this took the form of 'cabinets of curiosity' or 'Wunderkammer' exhibiting collections of natural and man-made objects in the houses of the European elites.

However, in terms of our understanding of the role of objects in human lives, there are some important works of theory that have described in fundamental terms not only how humans value objects but also how objects influence humans. For one, the German socialist thinker Karl Marx, within his broader analysis of economic structures and power relationships, addressed the particular values placed on material things by humans. It is in Marx's nineteenth-century analysis of capitalist society that we see objects most clearly as 'commodities' and this has been influential in subsequent scholarship on objects and material culture.[1] Marx acknowledged two main values placed upon objects: firstly, their usefulness and, secondly, their value when exchanged for money. In this framework, the object's usefulness is measured by its ability to meet specific human wants or needs, and its 'use-value' is something intrinsic to it. However, objects have another value – their 'exchange-value' – which calculates what one object is worth in relation to another, and this value is determined by a complex range of variables. Marx questioned the dominance of the exchange or monetary value of things in capitalist societies and suggested instead that the amount of labour that is dedicated to creating a given object should be the pre-eminent determinant of its value. Clearly, Marx's discussion of objects as commodities forms one part of his wider analysis of capitalism as a socio-economic framework, but within this context issues of social and cultural value are also addressed. For Marx, humans do not have social relationships with objects but they sometimes appear as if they do, and he proposed 'commodity fetishism' as an explanation for how humans can perceive economic value as something intrinsic to the object. For Marx, the market exchange of objects represents a process that actively obscures the relations of production between workers and their bosses and, as a consequence, deceives individuals about the economic structures that shape their lives. The influence of Marxist thought on twentieth-century scholarship is hard to over-estimate. However, for some scholars working in the early twentieth century, objects were not mere commodities but could have a much more varied range of meanings.

In the 1920s, two European anthropologists conducted research into societies very different from their own and developed theories which saw objects as having important social (rather than economic) relations.[2] During the First World War, Polish anthropologist Bronisław Malinowski spent several years on the Trobriand Islands in Melanesia, and the results of his ethnographic work on the Islanders were published in *Argonauts of the Western Pacific* in 1922.[3] It was in Malinowski's description of the 'Kula ring' – a form of gift-giving – that the notion of a 'gift economy' as opposed to a market economy was first articulated in full.[4] Malinowski had observed that the Trobriand Islands were a place of relative plenty and, yet, the Islanders chose to engage in gift-giving activities. Malinowski was curious to find out about what defined wealth in this society and what might motivate people to exchange things. His key findings centred on the reciprocity that was engendered by gift-giving. In other words, Malinowski observed a range of different kinds of gift-giving but found that the expectation of receiving some gift in return was common to almost all of them. In the 'Kula' system, it was expected that after a gift had been bestowed on another person, a gift of equivalent value would be returned at a later date and, in the meantime, smaller gifts might be issued in recognition of the obligation until a gift of the appropriate value could be offered. This observation led Malinowski to argue that gift-giving was a social act and, in this context, the gifting conferred status on the gift-giver rather than on the person who received the gift. Often gifts were given which were not needed (e.g. a gift of a yam when the recipient already had plenty of yams), but the act of giving placed the recipient in a position of obligation to the gift-giver. The giving of the gift, therefore, affected power relationships and generated a dynamism in social ties within Trobriand communities. In this case study, objects were not valuable simply for their inherent usefulness or for their economic value, but were used instead to develop social bonds of obligation and to confer prestige on the giver and a sense of reciprocal duty on the recipient. It was, however, Malinowski's debate with the French anthropologist Marcel Mauss which led to the full development of the concept of 'gift exchange' in anthropology.[5]

Marcel Mauss's *The Gift* (1925) has been highly influential in anthropologists' approach to the study of material culture. Like Malinowski, Mauss investigated non-European societies in Melanesia, Polynesia and the Pacific North-West.[6] Mauss's work developed the concept of the gift in societal terms, focusing on its active and constitutive role within a complex network of social relations and organisations. In other words, Mauss illuminated the gift as an active force within society and one that contributed to the quality and characteristics of human relationships. The results of Mauss's and Malinowski's ethnographies of Melanesian societies was a distillation of a range of different forms of exchange that could be observed in society and also the importance of reciprocity within gift-giving culture. Both anthropologists also sought to use their analysis of so-called 'primitive' societies to show that the cultures of these peoples were no less sophisticated than European culture. Moreover, they demonstrated that features of gift-giving were highly present within Western society, past and present. In terms of object-based research, Malinowksi and Mauss laid the foundations for subsequent thinkers to advance the concept of objects having agency in human lives, a break-through that remains at the forefront of material culture studies today.

Object agency

The philosophical concepts of 'subject' and 'object' have provided an enduring conceptual framework for the ways in which we think about physical objects in relation to ourselves. In these terms, the subject has consciousness and unique personal experiences; meanwhile, the object is the thing that might be observed and defined by the subject. This perceived division between subject and object in terms of their relative agency – or capacity to act – in the world has been influential. Philosophers and theorists of the twentieth century have overturned this way of thinking and advanced the idea that material objects themselves can be actors. For example, the German philosopher Martin Heidegger in his 1927 work *Being and Time* (which was published in English for the first time in 1962) outlined a different way of thinking about objects and 'being'.[7] In his famous 'tool analysis', Heidegger denied the reality of objects as entities in themselves and posited instead that objects are only meaningful in relation to other objects and persons. He observed that, in many circumstances, an object only presents itself to a person – becomes 'present-at-hand' – when it ceases to perform the function for which it is intended. In other words, it is the moment when the handle of the teapot breaks, rendering the object inadequate to its task, that we first actually come to notice the teapot. Working on this basis, the philosopher Graham Harman has developed his 'object-oriented philosophy', which ultimately rejects the primacy of human agency over the agency of objects.[8] Harman's work offers a re-thinking of the object–subject divide, but there have been other significant contribu-tions that have added to the argument that objects – far from being inactive and inarticulate – do in fact act and even 'speak'.

In the 1970s the French anthropologist and philosopher Pierre Bourdieu showed how everyday goods are capable of socialising the young – for Bourdieu, identities were formed not only through interactions with other people but also with foods, furniture or clothing.[9] Bourdieu focused especially on the way that objects were arranged within the home and the influence these spatial and material arrangements had on childhood development. Building on these ideas, Bruno Latour – himself a social scientist – analysed the laboratory as the environment in which 'science' is practised.[10] Latour contends that the production of scientific knowledge cannot be disentangled from its material and social contexts and places emphasis on the role of people and things in the production of science. More recently, Latour and colleagues developed their influential Actor Network Theory, which argues that agency is shared between humans and things, each one capable of acting upon the other.[11] In this world, objects occupy roles within social networks and are capable of active participation in such networks. Latour's work has opened the gates for new and experimental approaches to the study of 'things', a good example being Lorraine Daston's *Things that Talk*.[12] Published in 2004, this book challenges the characterisation of objects as mute by claiming that they are as talkative as we are ourselves. This collection of essays takes a playful approach to engaging with Heideggerian and Latourian thought and also with an academic culture which routinely speaks for 'things' rather than allowing things to speak for themselves. Together, these works have shown that for those of us who wish to study objects, assumptions about the way humans and non-humans interact are too easily made. They make it clear that developing an awareness of the ways in which objects act on human lives (as well as vice versa) can help researchers analyse both the material and the cultural.

OBJECT-CENTRED DISCIPLINES

Whilst material culture studies are widely acknowledged as resisting conventional disciplinary boundaries,[13] there are stronger traditions of researching artefacts within subjects such as archaeology, anthropology and art history than there are in others. Curatorial practice and expertise are also fundamental to our understanding of material culture, and whilst some curators work within particular disciplinary environments, such as ethnography or geology, this field is united by its absolute focus on the artefacts themselves. As such, the approaches taken by researchers in these areas have been influential and will be summarised here.

Archaeology

As a discipline, archaeology grew out of the antiquarian research of the eighteenth and nineteenth centuries that was gaining recognition with the founding of substantial national institutions such as the Society of Antiquaries (1707) and the British Museum (1753).[14] Early, but significant, excavations alongside the development of the science of geology allowed nineteenth-century archaeologists to begin to establish the antiquity of humankind.[15] The publication of Darwin's *On the Origin of the Species* in 1859 helped to consolidate the view that the history of humankind stretched much further back than the Bible suggested.[16] By the late nineteenth century, archaeology had developed systematic methods of analysis with a strong focus on fieldwork and the study of material culture found in excavations. Individuals such as William Flinders Petrie[17] set new standards in terms of the rigour of his excavations and the thorough way in which he documented his findings. Moreover, Petrie's meticulous work with excavated pottery led to the development of his Sequence Dating System, which used pottery styles as a key to dating archaeological sites (and, therefore, other objects).

From the late nineteenth until the mid-twentieth century, archaeologists were mainly concerned with chronology and with characterising the development of culture in different regions of the world. This period also saw close working relationships between archaeologists and anthropologists, both disciplines being focused on the classification of material found in the field.[18] Field techniques were greatly enhanced by pioneers such as Sir Mortimer Wheeler and Dorothy Garrod, and a new focus on the role of environment and ecology in the development of human culture was developed by archaeologists such as Grahame Clarke. By the end of the Second World War, new scientific techniques were beginning to be applied within archaeology and by the early 1960s the impact of inventions such as radiocarbon dating had transformed the discipline. However, in the 1960s and 1970s archaeology was changing. Some scholars in the field had begun to question the way that archaeology explained its findings and also the value of some of its interpretations. The 'New Archaeology' of this period moved the emphasis from describing the nature of culture in the past towards explaining it using logical scientific reasoning.[19] Society could be thought about as a series of systems and sub-systems, which – if analysed systematically – could help the researcher understand the culture as a whole.[20] This new approach, which allied scientific techniques with a scientific philosophy of enquiry, moved archaeology away from its interest in the study of individual objects or groups of things, and increasingly placed emphasis on 'pattern recognition'. This meant that the study of objects 'was reduced to artefact counts as whole sites were lumped into single assemblages as part of "quantification"'.[21] This trend, according to Miller et al., 'cast a shadow over anyone working on chronologies, typologies, a single group of artifacts, or in-depth studies of production technology'.[22]

Later in the twentieth century, and mirroring developments in other fields, some archaeologists argued in favour of a more plural approach to research – including a greater variety of methods and allowing a range of possible interpretations.[23] Today, elements of this later 'interpretive' or 'post-processual' approach exist alongside methods that are strongly scientific in character. However, over recent years, archaeologists – like anthropologists and historians – have revived their interest in the role of objects in the development of human relationships and cultures. To this end, the most common methods can be roughly categorised as follows: material analysis, classification and behavioural studies. The first is focused on the site and the objects excavated there, and aims to date individual artefacts (owing much to Petrie's Sequence Dating System). This approach attends to the life-cycle of an individual object – thinking through the history of an artefact from the sourcing of its raw materials to use and disposal – and interpreting it for social, cultural and economic insights.[24] The second approach – classification – emphasises the organisation of materials and makes use of pre-defined criteria in order to classify an object or group of objects. Finally, archaeologists also engage in behavioural studies, which seek to use material culture as evidence of past human action and patterns of behaviour. This approach often focuses upon the function or use of an object. Like material analysis, behavioural studies are also interested in the different stages the object may have been through, especially in relation to production and the technologies used in this process. This last approach relies heavily on the evidence of the first two approaches to form its conclusions.[25] Considering the wide range of analytical methods commonly used by archaeologists and their enduring interest in objects from the past rather than the present, this discipline has much to offer historians who are drawn to the study of material culture.

Anthropology

As we have seen, some of anthropology's early, seminal, work was conducted on the topic of gifts and gift-exchange. Simultaneously, the expansion of European empires led to the acquisition of vast quantities of material culture from across the world. The analysis and interpretation of such material were important features of the development of anthropology in the late nineteenth and early twentieth centuries and consolidated the discipline's connection with museums. Early ethnography conducted on indigenous communities in North America and elsewhere was also influenced by Darwin's theory of evolution. In the late nineteenth and early twentieth centuries, many anthropologists sought to study different human societies in order to trace 'cultural evolution', which saw hunting and gathering as 'primitive' and industrial, Western society as 'civilised'. However, work by key figures such as Franz Boas undermined this evolutionary perspective and advanced an empirical approach to research that valued the role of the environment, or nurture, in the development of human behaviour. Boas's students would produce some of the most important and popularly read works of twentieth-century anthropology, including Margaret Mead's *Coming of Age in Samoa* (1928) and Ruth Benedict's *The Chrysanthemum and the Sword: Patterns of Japanese culture* (1946).[26]

During the twentieth century, theoretical anthropology and material-based studies continued to develop, the latter flourishing within ethnographic museums.[27] However, in the late 1970s and 1980s it was the 'commodity' that made an important impact on the direction of travel for anthropological material culture studies. In 1979 anthropologist Mary Douglas teamed up with economist Baron Isherwood to write *The World of Goods: Towards a cultural anthropology of consumption,* which argued that consumption needed to be recognised as an integral part of our social system.[28] Following on from this work, Arjun Appadurai's *The Social Life of Things: Commodities in cultural perspective* further broke down the stigma that had evolved around understandings of the 'commodity' as a product of capitalist societies and mass consumption and, as such, not of primary interest to anthropologists who were focused on the study of non-Western societies.[29] The Marxist conceptualisation of the commodity had influenced anthropology, which came to view commodities as part of a process which saw the 'destruction of embedded customary relations, and the opening up of small-scale societies to market forces and capitalism'.[30] In contrast, Appadurai's edited collection helped to re-frame capitalism as a cultural (as well as economic) system worthy of anthropological study and positioned commodities within capitalism as having complex and changing social meanings.

Igor Kopytoff's essay, in particular, on the 'cultural biography of things' shows the value of asking the same questions of objects that we would ask of people and states that: 'A culturally informed economic biography of an object would look at it as a culturally constructed entity, endowed with culturally specific meanings, and classified and reclassified into culturally constituted categories.'[31] This work rehabilitated the study of consumption for a range of disciplines, shifting the focus from production and labour[32] to habits of consumption and use. Moreover, *The Social Life of Things* sought to place the 'things' themselves at the centre of the debate, and argued that:

> We have to follow the things themselves, for their meanings are inscribed in their forms, their uses, their trajectories. It is only through the analysis of these trajectories that we can interpret the human trans-actions and calculations that enliven things. Thus, even though from a theoretical point of view human actors encode things with signifi-cance, from a methodological point of view it is the things-in-motion that illuminate their human and social context.[33]

Appadurai's call to scholars to follow the trajectories of objects in their research is often cited and remains influential across a range of humanities and social science subjects. Moreover, moving on from the commodity as a defining concept for material culture studies has birthed a generation of anthropological scholarship which takes a more ethno-graphic approach to the study of objects. A good example of this trend is Daniel Miller's work on material culture, which includes *Material Culture and Mass Consumption* (1987) and *Material Cultures: Why some things matter*, which was published a decade later, amongst many other important con-tributions by Miller to material culture studies.[34] Miller's research and writing have also had a significant impact beyond the realms of anthro-pology, most especially in terms of his argument that thinking through material culture can help us to better understand social relations. However, following the objects themselves is not the dominant approach within historical studies of material culture. For this kind of research, we must look to art historical and curatorial approaches to object study.

Art history

'Material culture' encompasses the full spectrum of objects created by humans and of course includes those regarded as works of art. Jules Prown creates a useful distinction between 'art' and 'artefact' by considering the former as conscious creations which seek to communicate – whether to inform, influence, move, intimidate, impress, convert or persuade.[35] As a discipline, the history of art was one of the first scholarly traditions to place material things at its heart. As most art historians now consider art as an expression of the society and culture which produced it, their work is fundamentally important to historians of material culture.[36]

In the Western tradition, one of the earliest figures to trace the evolution of art was Giorgio Vasari, an artist and architect himself, but now better known as a significant pioneer 'art historian' with his publication on *The Lives of the Artists* (1550, much expanded in the second edition of 1568).[37] In his interpretation, the development of art was a cyclical process which had reached an earlier apex in the achievements of ancient Greece and Rome. He believed art had then gone into decline, only to be revived again in Italy in the fourteenth century, and was in the process of reaching another highpoint in the works of his near contemporaries, especially Michelangelo. His judgements were based upon his subjective aesthetic ideals, while his extensive biographical researches brought the figure of the creative artist into the foreground. His interpretations have been influential, as have been the insights he offered into the working practices of his contemporaries. Vasari highlighted painting, sculpture and architecture as the central practices of the artist, marginalising other media such as tapestries, metalwork, glass and ceramics.

Art theory was introduced into European academies in the mid-eighteenth century, with studies based around their universal ideal of beauty, rather than an attempt to study the historical significance of a work of art. Analysis of art with a genuinely historical standpoint was developed critically through the work of the German philosopher G. W. F. Hegel. Amongst his various important philosophical works, and during lectures he gave in the 1820s, Hegel articulated ideas about aesthetics. For Hegel, art represented the expression of spiritual freedom. Using examples ranging from India to the Low Countries, he posited that there were three fundamental stages in the development of art within any given culture that fitted with his Absolute Idea: the Symbolic (yet to achieve ideal beauty), the classical (works of ideal beauty) and the Romantic (those that go beyond ideal beauty towards inward experience). These theories prompted many debates, in particular about how changes in art occurred, whether it can be considered in a developmental sequence, and how different cultures developed specific forms of art.

Among those who challenged Hegel were scholars known as connoisseurs. Connoisseurship is another significant movement that critically influenced the development of art history in the nineteenth and twentieth centuries through figures such as Karl Friedrich von Rumohr, Giovanni Morelli and Bernard Berenson, although its origins can be traced back to Vasari. In contrast to philosophical and historical approaches, connoisseurial methods involve a close examination of the technique, medium, scale and condition of an artwork to judge its authenticity and attribution. Such scholars intensely debated which techniques bore the hallmarks of individual artists and how to categorise these systems of description. Connoisseurial analysis developed the language and terminology for describing artistic technique and form. It was fundamental in establishing the way in which art history was written in the nineteenth century, becoming recognised as a scholarly discipline that concentrated on the identification of art through visual analysis and attributing works to a particular artist. While the name 'connoisseurship' has acquired associations with elitism, empirical analysis, detailed description and identification of style are invaluable to historians of material culture as well as to art dealers and museum curators.

There have been many subsequent movements in art history, such as formalism, which broadened the question of style beyond individual artists to consider the style of epochs and cultures. Aby Warburg and Erwin Panofsky pioneered the study of iconography, revealing the layers of meaning present in the subjects depicted in works of art. Other developments in the study of art grew from wider political and scholarly trends. Marxist and social historians made an important contribution to the discipline of art history by asserting that art is fundamentally influenced by economic and historical forces. The so-called 'New Art History' of the 1970s and 1980s used literary theory such as deconstruction and semiotics, drawing attention to the flexibility of interpretation and the need to consider the perspective of the critic or viewer. Although some empirical and positivist studies continue to strive for the objective analysis of documentary and visual evidence, it is now generally recognised that art cannot be studied from a neutral standpoint – all analysis of the past, whether through images or text, is informed by the present concerns of the scholar or viewer. Feminism and post-colonial theory, which responded to the need in the second half of the twentieth century to challenge dominant narrative voices in history, have introduced yet further approaches to art history. Works of art can therefore be constantly reinterpreted with new approaches and analytical frameworks informed by both previous scholarship and present concerns.

Several themes underpinning the discipline of art history are pertinent to historians using material culture. Examining iconography (i.e. the intended meaning of the subject matter) offers compelling opportunities for comparative studies of symbolism and interpretation between the works of artists and across time. The question of patronage is also critical in informing an art historian's understanding of a work. For example, commissions often included specifications of the content of a painting, information which allows art historians to establish the parameters in which individual artists were able to express themselves. Much European art prior to the sixteenth century was commissioned by, or for, religious institutions and depicted religious subjects. Churches, monasteries or abbeys engaged artists to adorn their buildings while secular patrons commissioned chapels or devotional works for their homes. Another important strand is that of reception – how viewers perceived and received art. These social and cultural aspects of art history, beyond formal analysis, intersect with the work of cultural historians and historians of material culture.

Art history as taught in European and American universities has for many decades focused upon works in the Western tradition, whereas art from the wider world tended to be considered separately, as part of 'Oriental Studies' departments or – in the case of art from Africa, Oceania and the Americas – through anthropology departments. These disciplinary separations are gradually changing, with art history departments employing scholars working on world cultures and taking a global view. A key facet of art history is tracing the influence of different traditions upon artists by establishing how artistic ideas and forms travelled and were transmitted, an approach which has many commonalities with global history. A significant trend since the mid-1980s has been to expand the conventional geographical frame within which Western art has been considered to examine cultural influences from beyond Europe. Scholars are productively bringing these disciplines into closer dialogue by tracing the movement of objects and ideas around the world, along with their changing meanings and influence in different cultural contexts.[38]

Museums and curatorship

Museums have a duty of care towards their collections and part of this process focuses on the documentation of individual artefacts. Documentation helps to contextualise objects within their collections and also to explain their origins and histories – all of which makes objects more usable for the purposes of research, learning and engagement. In simple terms, the more a museum knows about the collections in their care, the better they are able to fulfil their obligations to look after objects and make them accessible to others. Curatorial research on material culture, therefore, can be divided roughly into three major concerns: firstly, with individual objects and their meanings; secondly, with the significance of the museum as an institution and keeper of objects; and, lastly, with the ways in which collections come to be formed, the relationships between objects and collections and broader issues connected with collecting, both historically and within contemporary society.[39] The latter subject is particularly important because museums as custodians of material culture have a strong interest in verifying the provenance of objects in their collections – to ensure that the legal status of the object in relation to the museum is clear.[40] Museums are also one of our principal repositories of primary source material and, thus, the study of museum objects necessitates an engagement with the reasons they came to be in that place and the meanings that gather around objects once they take up residence within a particular collection. Acknowledging these features of museum objects is important for more than one reason. In the first instance, assessing the reasons for an object's survival in the historical record is a standard feature of historical research practice and having some knowledge of the context of a primary source, in terms of the collection it sits within, can help the researcher to decipher its meanings. However, the need to engage with the context of a museum or collection runs deeper. Museums, like archives, mediate our experience of primary sources, but they do so in different ways. For historians to become adept in the field of material culture research, it is important to think through the museum as an institution and a place of study.

Museums revolve around the objects in their care; however, the work of a curator is not confined to the study of the objects in their collections but spans a wide range of other concerns, from the management and conservation of collections to display and education. Arguably, in recent decades, curators have found themselves with diminishing time and resource for research as demands increase upon them to engage diverse audiences, while many museums are starved of the funding they need.[41] However, it is the study of objects and their documentation that forms the basis of making collections more widely accessible to people outside of the institution. An object with no information can be a prompt to curiosity, but visitors still come to museums looking for answers more than mysteries. Nonetheless, with the enduring popularity of museum careers has come a broad range of university degrees dedicated to the study of museum practice and an army of textbooks outlining the theoretical frameworks within which we might understand the museum and the objects it contains.[42]

HISTORICAL MATERIAL CULTURES STUDIES: A NEW FIELD

Early modern and modern historians' interest in material culture emerged most clearly in the 1960s and 1970s alongside, and allied to, a growth in work on social history, 'history from below', women's history and the histories of indigenous peoples and enslaved communities.[43] While societies worldwide faced the post-colonial era and civil rights campaigns reached an apex in North America and elsewhere, academics became increasingly interested in studying marginalised groups in history.[44] These historical subjects had not necessarily left a textual record of their lives, action or thoughts. Moreover, where they had, their records had not been accorded the same value as others and were, therefore, much less likely to survive in archives or museums.[45] Even when records had been maintained, by luck or accident, they had been largely ignored by mainstream scholarship. It was this realisation in the mid- to late twentieth century that textual records did not hold all the answers for these new histories that led some historians to material culture.

The vanguard of this movement was in North America, where scholars had focused in particular on the subjects of folklore and indigenous communities in their region. In America after the Second World War, folklorists gained an institutional voice in the Pennsylvania Dutch Folklore Center and were able to push forward a research agenda that emphasised the material survivals of 'folklife'. In the 1970s the 'New Indian History' helped to legitimise the study of indigenous peoples by historians and began to correct the existing histories of America that cast native Americans as savages and the rightful losers in the fight for America's future. Moreover, this new scholarship recognised the lack of written histories in cultures that had strong alternative traditions for collective memory. As with the study of folk traditions or working-class cultures, oral histories and the study of cultural artefacts came to the fore. This movement towards the study of history through material culture received a further boost from a different quarter: the history of technology, whose practitioners increasingly saw American technology as the key to building a sense of a progressive 'national character' during the Cold War era.

Another important institution in the development of historical material culture studies, the Winterthur Museum in Delaware, saw its remit as establishing and enhancing knowledge of American cultural life and art. Their journal, the *Winterthur Portfolio*, sought from its first issue in 1964 to tell America's story through its decorative arts. These mid-century developments in the USA chimed with trends in the UK and Europe and created a research context within history that was more sympathetic to histories of the marginalised and the study of objects as opposed to texts. This would lead to the upsurge in material culture history publications of the late 1980s and 1990s, but this development did not happen cleanly or quickly. This so-called 'material turn' was influenced simultaneously by a range of parallel developments in historical studies, including the rise of cultural, as opposed to social, history and the shift from the study of 'women's history' to a broader 'gender history'.

Having discussed some of the traditions and challenges that exist within historical material culture studies, it is worth outlining what exactly material culture offers the historian as a primary source. Firstly, if we wish to be encompassing of human history then it is true to say that humans made tools before they wrote words and, therefore, the study of material culture opens up centuries of history that leave no textual record. This point, of course, leads to a more pertinent one for those historians and classicists studying Ancient civilisations through to the twentieth century: for most of history only a very small percentage of the population was literate and, therefore, most could not record their lives in writing. That is not to say that the lives of the illiterate are entirely absent from documentary sources, but they are rarely able to speak for themselves through these sources. The working poor in the medieval and early modern periods were sometimes the subjects of parish records or court cases but rarely are their own words left to posterity; more often, all that survives is a name, a date or a small detail of a life. This state of affairs also contrasts markedly with the quantity and quality of records left by the most wealthy and powerful in society. As Anne Gerritsen has commented, in her discussion of Jingdezhen ceramics and the community that made them, 'what we know is shaped by the limits of the extant sources, and where sources are compiled by members of the empire-wide elite … they can only reflect the perspective of the upper layers of society and culture'.[46]

Another important analytical advantage presented by the study of material culture is that it offers a method of understanding that is non-verbal and which accommodates the significance of tactile engagement with three-dimensional forms. Of course, the validity of this kind of 'sensory knowing' is open to debate, given the distance between us lighting a candle in the twenty-first century and a person doing the same in the fourteenth century. Nevertheless, historians of science and technology in particular have promoted this form of knowing, seeing and engagement with the materials and apparatus of science and technology as revealing of tacit knowledge. As John Kouwenhoven has commented: 'Words do not have meaning; they convey it.'[47] Things, in contrast, can be argued to both embody meaning and convey meaning. It is these facets of material culture research that offer historians something new and different and suggest that, rather than merely seeking to incorporate objects into historical research, historical research might benefit from responding to the distinct qualities of material as opposed to textual sources.

Despite these powerful arguments in favour of studying objects as well as texts, it is also worth acknowledging that the survival of material objects is mediated by many of the same forces that determine the contents of archives or libraries – prioritising the elite, the prized, the complete and the robust. Museum collections, by and large, do not deal so well in the ephemeral – which is quite often the best way to access marginalised lives. Sometimes 'material' worlds can only be made manifest through textual and visual sources. Even where relevant artefacts come easily to hand, historians will, for the most part, seek to combine this evidence with other sources. The key to making the most of material culture as a source for historical enquiry is to recognise the new avenues it can offer the historian but, at the same time, to apply all the same critical skills employed in the choice and analysis of more traditional primary sources.

THE STATE OF THE FIELD TODAY

A particular challenge for those seeking to understand this field of research is that the use of material sources is not evenly distributed across periods and genres of historical research. Whilst the study of material culture has traditionally been most well established amongst scholars of ancient and medieval history,[48] there has recently been some intense activity amongst social and cultural historians working on the early modern period (around 1500–1800). As an era of rapidly increasing production of domestic goods, eighteenth-century Britain has been extensively examined as an emerging consumer culture, with domestic furnishings and personal effects attracting particularly close scrutiny.[49] On the whole, social and cultural studies have been much quicker to incorporate objects, buildings and spaces into their analysis than have economic and political histories.[50] In particular, histories of women's lives have made excellent use of material things to locate female experience and agency in the context of patriarchal society and its reflections in the textual record.[51]

Of course, such emphases within existing literature have deepened our understanding of the cultural construction of identity, but also point to topics that remain largely disengaged from the study of material culture in particular for modern history. In 2009, Frank Trentmann made an assessment of historical material culture studies focused on the eighteenth and nineteenth centuries, suggesting that 'The historical embrace of things … has been partial.'[52] In particular, he highlights the fact that 'historical material culture studies have been more about culture than about material'.[53] Similarly, Giorgio Riello has commented on the lack of interest amongst historians in histories *of things* (such as the discovery of a novel example of a particular kind of artefact or the study of that artefact in its own right). Rather, he sees historians as being comfortable working on histories *from things* or, in other words, using objects as a category of primary source alongside more traditional forms of evidence.[54] To challenge this conservatism, Riello proposes an approach he terms 'history *and things*', which follows the lead of other disciplines, such as anthropology, in allowing material culture a role in shaping the questions we ask and the methods we use to analyse the past.[55]

Developments in neighbouring disciplines also feed into the mainstream of historical research on material culture. Within literary studies, for example, Peter Stallybrass has played a pioneering role in promoting interest in 'material texts',[56] enhancing our understanding of literary culture through attending to the material. For literary scholars, studying the materiality of text is revealing of how material form influences meaning, and the subject of materiality has prompted a range of reflective, critical and imaginative responses from scholars. This sub-field does not relate as strongly to material culture studies as it does to the history of the book, which has had a long-term interest in the physical manifestation of text. 'Material texts' is developing as a field of enquiry with increasing numbers of research centres, seminars and special subject series with publishers. This work promises to shed light on how many different kinds of text have been embodied and circulated in the past and, in this respect, literary scholars in this field share many of the same concerns as historians and historians of science. Also in the field of literature, Bill Brown's influential 'thing theory' introduced Heidegger's work on human–object relations to literary theory.[57]

Another important adjacent field of research is design history, which focuses attention on objects in terms of both their stylistic and historical contexts, most especially for twentieth-century artefacts and the products of mass production. However, in recent decades design historians have shifted from an approach that heavily prioritises the design process to embrace a broader range of issues relating to the production and consumption of objects and their roles in society. This encompassing perspective on the world of things has produced such works as Judy Attfield's *Wild Things: The material culture of everyday life* that pay attention to the quotidian and which acknowledge 'the physical object in all its materiality' encompassing 'the work of design, making, distributing, consuming, using, discarding, recycling and so on'.[58] Attfield and others have pushed their discipline to deal with messy everyday life in contrast to the 'pristine aesthetic objects' of design collections and have stressed that design can be located within diverse social contexts.

The interdisciplinary field of historical geography has also been fruitful for the study of material culture, and a productive dialogue exists between geographers and historians on the subjects of materiality and space.[59] Urban specialists, for example, have become preoccupied with the agency of the material world of the modern city.[60] A good example of this kind of historical geography is Alastair Owens's collaborative project with archaeologists on the material culture of everyday life in Victorian London.[61] An important contribution of this study is the use of an interpretive framework 'that considers what objects did for, as much as what they mean to, Victorian Londoners'.[62] Historical geographers, such as David Livingstone, have also explored the material and spatial dimensions of knowledge production[63] and questions of the material, embodied characteristics of expertise have preoccupied historians of science, seeking to elucidate connections between tacit and theoretical knowledge.[64] This research on space and the circulation of materials and ideas reveals new networks of connection that are not commonly visible in intellectual histories. Moreover, by foregrounding material things and their journeys, recent historical scholarship has been able to explore the passage and transmission of objects as a means by which different societies and economies were connected. In this way, the study of material culture in a range of historical contexts (geographical, technological or intellectual) has helped to develop global histories of the movement of objects and ideas.[65]

The history of collecting material culture and natural specimens is now a vibrant interdisciplinary field which at its core interrogates how humans have produced knowledge about the world around them.[66] Art historians and antiquarians initially undertook what is now known as collecting history by researching the provenance of works by great artists – for example, tracing the movement of paintings, drawings and sculpture from Italy purchased by members of the British elite during the Grand Tour in the seventeenth and eighteenth centuries. These studies often dealt with questions of attribution, for example finding evidence in the history of an artwork to establish whether or not it was created by a particular artist. While much of this work was confined to histories of connoisseurship and focused, to a large extent, on works of art in the European tradition, collecting history encompasses a much broader range of material culture from across the world. For example, substantial research has been carried out on the subject of early modern collecting and the history of 'cabinets of curiosities', which considers how such exotic objects found their way to Europe, who acquired them, how they were exchanged, in what quantities, and how they were displayed.[67] These studies use the histories of these objects and their collectors to make new observations about early modern society and culture.

Another important strand of research within the history of collecting sits at the intersection between imperial history and anthropology. As European nations established control over territory in the Americas, Asia, Africa and Oceania from the early modern period onwards, individuals including merchants, colonial officials, missionaries, soldiers and sailors collected material culture from indigenous peoples. Some collected these objects for their curiosity value, while missionaries often acquired objects from converts to Christianity as 'proof' of the success of their mission. Others, including colonial officers, collected material in order to better understand the societies of the people they were ruling – through the study of local laws, leadership, religions and customs. The categorisation of indigenous people became an important tool of imperialism and objects – such as clothing, adornment and weapons – became, alongside physical characteristics, critical evidence for identifying and classifying people into groups such as castes and tribes. The development of social and physical anthropology is, therefore, associated with this history of imperial expansion. By the late nineteenth and early twentieth century, as the discipline of anthropology was beginning to be established in universities, collecting by colonial officials represented an important source of material evidence which could be brought back to Britain and examined by scholars. In addition, anthropologists embarked on collecting expeditions of their own to imperial territories – to furnish their research with relevant artefacts of study.

The processes briefly described above have been an important part of the so-called 'new' imperial history, which pays attention to the culture of imperialism in order to understand the exertion of, challenges to and tensions within imperial power.[68] Such studies investigate the myriad forces and motivations underpinning the collection of objects in imperial settings, including the need to understand local populations to inform governance, gift exchange, 'preservation' of indigenous cultures, the imposition of power, aesthetic and scholarly concerns, and missionaries' use of objects to prove their 'civilising' successes. Attending to the moment of object and knowledge exchange also demonstrates the central role of local agents who were critical in the production of knowledge as donors, interpreters or collectors, and who had their own motivations for supporting collecting projects.

IN SUMMARY

Here we have provided an overview of the origins of material culture studies and the disciplinary specialisms that have the strongest bearing on their development. Moreover, we have considered the particular place of historical work within this context and the many potentialities material culture history might offer in the future. The next chapter will explain the process of planning and designing a research project, focusing on the work that can be done at an early stage to make the research both original and feasible.

NOTES

1 See K. Marx, *Das Kapital: Kritik der politischen Ökonomie* [Capital: Critique of political economy] vols 1–3 (Hamburg: Otto Meissner, 1867), pp. 85, 94.

2 Anthropology emerged as a discipline in the nineteenth century and represented an attempt to study human behaviour in a systematic way. However, early anthropology was deeply entangled with the colonial project and, as such, focused on 'primitive' peoples and promulgated theories of social evolution. By the first decades of the twentieth century, ethnography as a methodology was being developed and anthropologists such as Bronisław Malinowski were promoting 'immersion fieldwork' as a research strategy. See T. Hylland Eriksen and F. Sivert Nielsen, *A History of Anthropology* (London: Pluto Press, 2001).

3 B. Malinowski, *Argonauts of the Western Pacific: An account of native enterprise and adventure in the archipelagos of Melanesian New Guinea*, with a foreword by Adam Kuper (London: Routledge, 2014).

4 The classic text is M. Mauss, *The Gift: The form and reason for exchange in archaic societies* (London: Routledge, 2002).

5 For more information, see M. Gane (ed.), *The Radical Sociology of Durkheim and Mauss* (London: Routledge, 1992). Marcel Mauss was the nephew of sociologist and philosopher Émile Durkheim.

6 Unlike Malinowski, however, Mauss did not engage in fieldwork in these regions.

7 M. Heidegger, *Being and Time* (Oxford: Blackwell, 1962).

8 G. Harman, *Tool-Being: Heidegger and the metaphysics of objects* (Chicago: Open Court, 2002). Harman is joined by thinkers such as Ian Bogost in describing an 'object-oriented ontology'.

9 P. Bourdieu, *Outline of a Theory of Practice* (Cambridge: Cambridge University Press, 1977). His later work on consumption sees objects as having an important role in inculcating individuals into prevailing social norms and class distinctions; see P. Bourdieu, *Distinction: A social critique of the judgement of taste* (London: Routledge, 2010).

10 B. Latour and S. Woolgar, *Laboratory Life: The social construction of scientific facts* (London: Sage Publications, 1979).

11 B. Latour, *Reassembling the Social: An introduction to Actor-Network-Theory* (Oxford: Oxford University Press, 2005).
12 L. Daston, *Things that Talk: Object lessons from art and science* (New York: Zone, 2004).
13 See, for example, C. Tilley (ed.), *Reading Material Culture: Structuralism, hermeneutics and post-structuralism* (Oxford: Basil Blackwell, 1990), p. vii, and Schlereth, 'Material Culture Research', 22.
14 The Society of Antiquaries Scotland was founded in 1780 and the Royal Society of Antiquaries of Ireland in 1849.
15 Excavations included those at the sites of Pompeii and Herculaneum in modern day Italy. See C. Renfrew and P. Bahn, *Archaeology: Theories, methods and practice* (London: Thames & Hudson, 2016), pp. 21–6.
16 C. Darwin, *On the Origin of the Species* (London: Ward Lock & Co., 1911).
17 M. S. Drower, *Flinders Petrie: A life in archaeology* (London: Gollancz, 1985).
18 Renfrew and Bahn, *Archaeology*, p. 32.
19 This approach is often termed the 'processual tradition' and connects with the rise of 'structural functionalism' within philosophy and the social sciences.
20 Renfrew and Bahn, *Archaeology*, pp. 40–1.
21 G. L. Miller, O. R. Jones, L. A. Ross and T. Majewski, 'Approaches to Material Culture Research for Historical Archaeologists', in D. R. Brauner (ed.), *Approaches to Material Culture Research for Historical Archaeologists*, 2nd edn (Tuscon, AZ: Society for Historical Archaeology, 2000), pp. 1–10, p. 1.
22 Ibid.
23 This shift away from the notion of absolute objectivity in archaeological research was influenced by the concept of 'relativism'.
24 C. Gosden and Y. Marshall, 'The Cultural Biography of Objects', *World Archaeology*, 31:2 (1999), 169–78.
25 Brauner, *Approaches to Material Culture*, pp. 2–6.
26 M. Mead, *Coming of Age in Samoa* (Harmondsworth: Penguin Books, 1943); R. Benedict, *The Chrysanthemum and the Sword: Patterns of Japanese culture* (London: Routledge & Kegan Paul, 1964).
27 H. Kuklick (ed.), *The New History of Anthropology* (Oxford: Blackwell, 2008).
28 M. Douglas and B. Isherwood, *The World of Goods: Towards a cultural anthropology of consumption* (London: Allen Lane, 1979).
29 A. Appadurai (ed.), *The Social Life of Things: Commodities in cultural perspective* (Cambridge: Cambridge University Press, 1986).

30   D. Miller, 'Consumption and Commodities', *Annual Review of Anthropology*, 24 (1995), 141–61, p. 144.

31   I. Kopytoff, 'The Cultural Biography of Things: Commoditization as a cultural process', in Appadurai (ed.), *Social Life of Things*, pp. 64–91, p. 68.

32   Daniel Miller has reviewed literature across sociology, human geography and history from the 1950s to the 1970s and discovered that there was very little written about consumption, see D. Miller (ed.), *Acknowledging Consumption: A review of new studies* (London: Routledge, 1995). However, in this same period, there is intense investigation of the subject of labour and production, especially in history: see, for example, T. S. Aston, *The Industrial Revolution 1760–1830* (Oxford: Oxford University Press, 1948) and E. Hobsbawm, *Labouring Men: Studies in the history of labour* (London: Weidenfeld & Nicolson, 1964).

33   Appadurai, *Social Life of Things*, p. 5.

34   D. Miller, *Material Culture and Mass Consumption* (Oxford: Basil Blackwell, 1987); Miller (ed.), *Material Cultures: Why some things matter* (London: UCL Press, 1997).

35   J. D. Prown, 'The Truth of Material Culture: History or Fiction?', in S. D. Lubar and W. D. Kingery (eds), *History from Things: Essays on material culture* (Washington, DC: Smithsonian Institution Press, 1993), pp. 1–169, pp. 2–3. For Prown, artefacts such as utilitarian objects offer alternative insights into the beliefs and values of individuals and societies in the past by the very lack of self-consciousness in their production.

36   For a clear introduction to the development of the discipline, see: M. Hatt and C. Klonk, *Art History: A critical introduction to its methods* (Manchester: Manchester University Press, 1996).

37   G. Vasari, *The Lives of Artists*, translated with an introduction and notes by Julia Conaway Bondanella and Peter Bondanella (Oxford: Oxford University Press, 1991).

38   See, for example, A. Gerritsen and G. Riello (eds), *The Global Lives of Things: The material culture of connections in the early modern world* (London: Routledge, 2016). See also the special issue of *Art History* 38:4 (2015) edited by Meredith Martin and Daniela Bleichmar on 'Objects in Motion in the Early Modern World'.

39   Pearce, *Interpreting Objects*.

40   Most objects are the property of the museum in which they reside; however, in some cases objects might be on long-term loan from another collection or a private owner. Museums are required to hold documentation that details the provenance of an object not only to prove that it is a genuine artefact but also to show that it legally belongs to the museum.

41 See, for example, Museums Association, Annual Report 2015, 'Policy and Advocacy', p. 10: www.museumsassociation.org/download?id=1151014 [accessed 14 October 2015].

42 See, for example, S. MacDonald (ed.), *The Politics of Display: Museums, science, culture* (London: Routledge, 1998); R. Sandell (ed.), *Museums, Society, Inequality* (London: Routledge, 2002); S. Pearce (ed.), *Museums and the Appropriation of Culture* (London: Athlone Press, 1994); S. Dudley (ed.), *Museum Objects: Experiencing the properties of things* (London: Routledge, 2012).

43 Although there had been a consistent vein of scholarship focused on man-made objects that represented particularly fine technical and artistic skill, led by art historians and often described as the study of 'decorative arts'. See, for example, M. Snodin and J. Styles, *Design and the Decorative Arts: Britain 1500–1900* (London: V&A, 2001).

44 For explanations of these 'new' fields of interest see: J. W. Scott, 'Gender: A useful category of historical analysis', *The American Historical Review*, 91:5 (1986), 1053–75; M. Taylor, 'The Beginnings of Modern British Social History?', *History Workshop Journal*, 43 (1997), 155–76; R. F. Berhofer, 'The Political Context of a New Indian History', *Pacific Historical Review*, 40:3 (1971), 357–82.

45 Although it is worth noting late nineteenth- and early twentieth-century anthropological interest in 'native' or 'primitive' peoples, which led to the controversial form of collecting known as 'salvage ethnography', as practised by anthropologist Franz Boas, and also widespread collecting of the artefacts of indigenous cultures. See The Pitt Rivers Museum, Oxford: www.prm.ox.ac.uk [accessed 15 October 2015].

46 A. Gerritsen, 'Ceramics for Local and Global Markets: Jingdezhen's agora of technologies', in D. Schäfer (ed.), *Cultures of Knowledge: Technology in Chinese history* (Leiden: Brill, 2012), pp. 161–84, p. 183.

47 J. A. Kouwenhoven, 'American Studies: Words or things?' in T. J. Schlereth (ed.), *Material Culture Studies in America* (New York: Altamira Press, 1999), p. 84.

48 Interdisciplinary Medieval studies centres incorporating staff from art history, archaeology, history and literature departments have existed in British universities since the 1960s and have trained up several generations of historians who are adept in integrating material culture into their analysis.

49 See, for example, L. Weatherill, *Consumer Behaviour and Material Culture in Britain, 1660–1760* (London: Economic and Social Research Council, 1988); C. Shammas, *The Pre-Industrial Consumer in England and America* (Oxford: Clarendon, 1990); J. Styles and A. Vickery (eds), *Gender, Taste*

and Material Culture in Britain and North America (London: The Paul Mellon Centre for Studies in British Art, 2006); J. Hamlett, *Material Relations: Domestic interiors and middle-class families in England, 1850–1910* (Manchester: Manchester University Press, 2010).

50   There are notable exceptions, especially in relation to economic history, such as Giorgio Riello's work on material culture and trade. See, for example, G. Riello and T. Roy (eds), *How India Clothed the World: The world of south Asian textiles, 1500–1850* (Leiden: Brill, 2009).

51   See, for example, A. Vickery, 'His and Hers: Gender, consumption and household accounting in eighteenth-century England', *Past & Present – The Art of Survival: Gender and history in Europe, 1450–2000*, 1 (2006), 12–38, p. 13.

52   F. Trentmann, 'Materiality in the Future of History: Things, practices, and politics', *Journal of British Studies*, 48:2 (2009), 286.

53   Ibid., 288.

54   G. Riello, 'Things that Shape History: Material culture and historical narratives', in Harvey, *History and Material Culture*, pp. 24–47, p. 25.

55   Ibid., p. 26. Emphasis added here with use of italics on 'history *and things*'.

56   See A. Jones and P. Stallybrass (eds), *Renaissance Clothing and the Materials of Memory* (Cambridge: Cambridge University Press, 2000).

57   B. Brown, 'Thing Theory', *Critical Enquiry*, 28:1 (2001), 1–22.

58   J. Attfield, *Wild Things: The material culture of everyday life* (Oxford: Berg, 2000), p. 3.

59   See, for example, H. Lorimer, 'Cultural Geography: The busyness of being "more-than-representational"', *Progress in Human Geography*, 29:1 (2005), 83–94.

60   Tony Bennett and Patrick Joyce emphasise the agency of objects, and their role as a shaping force in history: 'the social … is seen to be performed by material things as much as by humans', P. Joyce and T. Bennett, 'Material Powers: Introduction', in T. Bennett and P. Joyce (eds), *Material Powers: Cultural studies, history and the material turn* (London: Routledge, 2010), pp. 1–22, p. 4. While Chris Otter argues: 'at certain points specific materials have played a pivotal role in constituting particular forms of the western urban system'. Otter, 'Locating Matter: The place of materiality in urban history', in Bennett and Joyce (eds), *Material Powers*, pp. 38–59, p. 46.

61   A. Owens, N. Jeffries, K. Wehner and R. Featherby, 'Fragments of the Modern City: Material culture and the rhythms of everyday life in Victorian London', *Journal of Victorian Culture*, 15:2 (2010), 212–25.

62   Ibid., 215.

63 D. N. Livingstone, 'Spaces of Knowledge: Contributions towards a historical geography of science', *Environmental Studies*, 13 (1995), 5–34.

64 Excellent examples include U. Klein and E. C. Spary, *Materials and Expertise in Early Modern Europe: Between market and laboratory* (Chicago: University of Chicago Press, 2010); C. Mukerji, *Impossible Engineering: Technology and territoriality on the Canal du Midi* (Princeton: Princeton University Press, 2009) and S. Werrett, 'Recycling in Early Modern Science', *British Journal for the History of Science*, 46 (2013), 122–38.

65 Telling global histories through an analysis of the movement of objects has become increasingly popular, as evinced in Giorgio Riello's recent work on the intercontinental exchange of commodities in the early modern period: Gerritsen and Riello, *Global Lives of Things*. Also see Margot Finn's research project on the East India Company in eighteenth- and nineteenth-century Britain, which places the decoration and furnishing of country houses in the context of trade and the burgeoning British Empire: http://blogs.ucl.ac.uk/eicah [accessed 19 January 2016].

66 S. M. Pearce, *On Collecting: An investigation into collecting in the European tradition* (London: Routledge, 1995); J. Elsner and R. Cardinal (eds), *The Cultures of Collecting* (London: Reaktion, 1994); A. Shelton (ed.), *Collectors: Expressions of self and other* (London: Horniman Museum, 2001); A. MacGregor, *Curiosity and Enlightenment: Collectors and collections from the sixteenth to the nineteenth century* (New Haven, CT: Yale University Press, 2007).

67 K. Sloan and A. Burnett (eds), *Enlightenment: Discovering the world in the eighteenth century* (London: British Museum Press, 2005); D. Bleichmar and P. C. Mancall (eds), *Collecting Across Cultures: Material exchanges in the early modern Atlantic world* (Philadelphia, PA: University of Pennsylvania Press, 2011).

68 Pioneering work by scholars such as Nicholas Thomas have successfully combined the history of anthropology with imperial history to develop our understanding of the 'entanglements of empire'. See N. Thomas, *Entangled Objects: Exchange, material culture, and colonialism in the Pacific* (Cambridge, MA: Harvard University Press, 1991); A. J. M. Henare, *Museums, Anthropology and Imperial Exchange* (Cambridge: Cambridge University Press, 2005).

RECOMMENDED FURTHER READING

Appadurai, Arjun (ed.), *The Social Life of Things: Commodities in cultural perspective* (Cambridge: Cambridge University Press, 1986).

Daston, Lorraine, *Things that Talk: Object lessons from art and science* (New York: Zone, 2004).

Latour, Bruno, *Reassembling the Social: An introduction to Actor-Network-Theory* (Oxford: Oxford University Press, 2005).

Miller, Daniel (ed.), *Material Cultures: Why some things matter* (London: UCL Press, 1997).

Pearce, Susan M. (ed.), *Interpreting Objects and Collections* (London: Routledge, 1994).

Schlereth, Thomas J., 'Material Culture Research and Historical Explanation', *The Public Historian* 7:4 (1985), 21–36.

❋ 2 ❋

PLANNING A RESEARCH PROJECT

In Chapter 1 we considered how different disciplines approach the study of the material world and traced its role within historical practice. In this chapter, we will look at strategies for developing effective research projects using material culture. First, we focus on initiating your project, then on how to formulate effective research questions. We then discuss a range of issues that affect the design of your project, followed by four case studies, and conclude with guidance on creating a realistic research schedule. Putting these foundations in place will greatly enhance your ability to develop an original research project which is achievable in the time available. Chapter 3 will move on to consider the methodologies that can help you develop this research to the full.

CONCEIVING YOUR PROJECT

To provide focus and structure, historians often organise their research into projects. While your aim might not be to write a book, the process of creating a research project is mirrored at all levels of historical practice. The advice here introduces effective strategies for conceiving and developing research projects using material culture as a source, for which the outcomes might be an extended essay, seminar paper, poster, dissertation, exhibition or website. This guidance recommends good research practice that you will find relevant throughout your historical studies and beyond.

As we have seen, there are many different approaches to studying material culture and they are closely related to the questions you seek to answer. Outlined below are two alternative starting points: the first describes a scenario where you know the period or theme you wish to explore; the second focuses on a project which is principally motivated by a broader interest in material culture. These cases are at opposite ends of the spectrum of scenarios for initiating a research project: it is, of course, more probable that your project will emerge from somewhere between these two points – for example, if you have a particular theme and a set of objects in mind.

Your research project should begin with scrutiny of a range of historical material prior to fixing upon specific research questions. As with all historical studies, a good understanding of the secondary literature is crucial and informs where original contributions to the field can be made. As you move on to assessing potential primary sources, carefully record where you find material, perhaps in a spreadsheet, noting the repository, database, accession numbers or classmarks and short descriptions of each source. You may build up a long list of sources before finalising your line of enquiry, but you will save time later by knowing what is located where. The number of objects studied depends on the research questions and methodology, so this is not simply a question of quantity but one of organisation and project design.

WHEN THE PERIOD OR THEME IS YOUR STARTING POINT

For students involved in undergraduate or postgraduate courses, it is often the case that a research project or essay based on primary sources represents the culmination of a programme of study. Programmes or modules of study are usually based around a period, geographical setting and/or theme. As you approach a more substantial piece of research, you may already have identified an angle or sub-theme of the course that has particularly inspired you. An example of a study that takes a theme as its subject and uses objects as supporting evidence might be research on soldiers' experiences of trench life during the First World War. A wide range of primary sources exists for this subject, but an innovative angle might be provided by using objects alongside poems, diaries, news reports and other written and visual sources to offer new perspectives on consumption, communication, the sensory and affective experience of soldiers' lives in the trenches, and war memory and legacy. A recent edited volume *Matters of Conflict: Material culture, memory and the First World War*, demonstrated a variety of objects and approaches to study – from mortar shells, trench art and soldiers' personal items to prosthetic limbs.[1]

If you are struggling to identify relevant material culture to use in your analysis of a wider historical theme, it is worthwhile reviewing the primary and secondary literature to assess the presence of objects within these texts. Objects – whether 'artefacts', ephemera or the materials of everyday life – might be mentioned in the secondary literature even if they do not take centre stage in the analysis. You can also make a point of looking at any illustrations included and think about whether these objects have been sufficiently analysed within the secondary literature. If you believe they have not been and could be used more productively, this might provide a viable starting point and help you to present new perspectives upon existing literature. This strategy has the added benefit that the literature should indicate in the captions or bibliography where these objects are located, providing you with a lead to follow up. However, it is worth remembering that once you have located some objects, you will still need to look for others to ensure that your source base is adequate (see Chapter 3 for guidance on methodology and Chapter 4 for locating primary sources).

If there are no obvious avenues from the secondary literature, it is worth thinking through the topic and asking yourself which kinds of objects might enlighten the theme. In the absence of historical work using material culture, it could also be useful to examine literature from other disciplines which may have incorporated the study of objects – such as archaeology, art history or anthropology – to see whether this subject has been analysed elsewhere. Visual images, such as paintings and photographs of the period in question, often depict relevant objects (as well as being objects themselves), and therefore enable you to identify potential subjects of study. Written primary sources from the period (including diaries, inventories and even fiction) can also indicate the presence of objects within past societies and allude to their possible meanings. The next step is to consider where examples of these objects might be located. Surveying the online collections of thematic museums (such as the Imperial War Museum, the Museum of English Rural Life or the National Maritime Museum) can prompt ideas about the kinds of objects that have survived relating to these topics.

WHEN THE MATERIAL SOURCES ARE YOUR STARTING POINT

In some cases, a particular object or set of objects might provide the inspiration for a research project. As noted above, you must consult secondary literature to establish which scholars have researched these types of objects and how they approached them, in order to work out where gaps in the analysis lie. In these circumstances, you may know the whereabouts of the material or, if it is an object type, where the most important examples of it are located. Even if you already know the location of the examples you wish to focus upon, it will still be important to use the research strategies outlined above to establish where other similar material might be stored. Are your chosen objects a discrete sample of the extant material, or are they unique examples of a particular type of artefact? Again, a rigorous methodology will require that you consider whether, for example, these objects were widely reproduced and, where possible, to locate further examples for the purposes of comparison. Research on the subject of Chinese porcelain imported into eighteenth-century Britain, focusing on the influence of these objects upon social practice and food culture, is a good example of a study that uses a type of material culture as its starting point. In this case, the specific genre of object is the main subject of study. Such a project is likely to involve an examination of the evidence of production, and the quantity and type of porcelain present in one or more collections in combination with analysis of references to the use of porcelain in contemporary written or visual sources.

There are, of course, many different starting points for research projects. The guidance here is relevant for developing an extended piece of writing or dissertation, as well as for smaller projects such as seminar presentations, posters or essays. Even if you are undertaking a small-scale project, thinking through the range of information you can interpret from your sources will set you up well for a broad range of possible questions in presentations.

FORMULATING RESEARCH QUESTIONS

As we discussed in the previous chapter, scholars from many disciplines have been drawn to the study of material culture. However, despite the use of very similar material sources, the questions that we ask of the material and the insights we wish to expose set our disciplines apart. As Gerritsen and Riello remind us: 'The engagement and usefulness of material culture depends upon the questions that we ask.'[2] Different motivations drive the work of art historians and literary scholars, curators and historical geographers. However, being aware of the debates in other disciplines can help historians in framing their own questions.

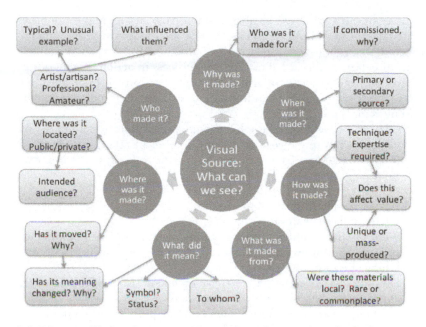

2.1 Diagram illustrating range of questions that can be asked of an object, and subsequent avenues to pursue.

Here, we will draw on a range of scholarship to make the process of formulating historical enquiries as transparent as possible.

Developing realistic and meaningful research questions is achieved through a series of preliminary investigations into the topic and the existing literature. Any extended piece of writing, whether a dissertation, thesis or book, will at its core respond to a series of two or three research questions. Not only is this the process by which historians shape their arguments, but you may be asked to present your research plan to a supervisor or fellow students in the form of a project summary, usually based around pre-defined research questions and a stated methodology. These should be compelling, original and feasible.

Research questions locate the project within scholarship and make clear the contribution the study will make to the existing literature. The larger over-arching questions help the scholar move a project from being a descriptive historical story or presentation of a set of data to an analytical enquiry. Your project will also involve smaller investigative questions but you should be able to stand back and highlight the principal questions you will be asking. Objects are capable of prompting an incredible variety of questions, each of which might take you in a different direction. Figure 2.1 illustrates this process in action. If your study starts with one object or a group of objects, it is worth brainstorming as many questions as you can think of, to explore the range of possible avenues for research.

Once you have decided upon a theme, period, location and a set of sources, you can refine your research questions by asking 'so what?' of your chosen material. To break this down – the following questions can be helpful:

- Why is this significant and to whom?
- What are these examples exemplary of?
- What do these findings reveal about larger historical phenomena such as continuity and change, cause and consequence, cultural interaction or quotidian experience?
- How will this research shed new light on major historical themes such as power, gender, race, identity and class?
- How important are different factors in shaping these phenomena? What existing explanations will be challenged or enhanced, and how will this project advance the debate?

Consider too the scale of the questions: they must not be so narrow that they do not speak to larger historical concerns, but they also need to be sufficiently directed to be feasibly answered within the scope of the project. Anything between one and three broad research questions can usefully shape a dissertation or extended essay and, in the case of studies using material culture as a significant part of the enquiry, it can also be appropriate to include an explicitly methodological question about the role of objects in the research. This methodological question can help to underline the originality of the approach and clarify the reasons behind your selection of primary sources. Remain mindful of what material culture does well: for example, giving voice to the kinds of historical experience which can best be judged through things, their production, display, value, exchange and use.

One object: many questions

As mentioned above, in considering how different disciplines approach material things a key difference lies in the questions they ask. Here, we will use a single object to illuminate the variation in questions and strategies for analysis that are commonly employed by historians and art historians. The painting in question is one that relates strongly to the study of material culture in that it depicts, alongside the sitter, a collection of objects. This exercise is designed to make explicit the sometimes subtle differences in approach and also to highlight the ways in which a single object can prompt diverse interpretations. We deliberately suggest a wide range of questions to demonstrate the rich possibilities for research emanating from a single object. In reality you would not be expected to cover all these angles and you would refine your enquiry down to two or three key questions depending on the available sources and the scope of the study. The remaining chapters will discuss strategies for answering these questions.

Benjamin West, a leading Anglo-American artist of the late eighteenth and early nineteenth centuries, painted a portrait of Joseph Banks – scientist, explorer and collector – on his return in 1771 from his voyage to the Pacific and South Sea islands on board Captain James Cook's ship HMS *Endeavour*.* In a full-length portrait (Figure 2.2), West depicts Banks surrounded by objects he collected during the expedition, his fingers gesturing towards the fabric of the Tahitian cloak that he is wearing. Other objects include Māori weapons, a Tahitian head-dress and a volume of botanical drawings. He stands in front of a classical column with a damask curtain drawn to one side. This image is therefore of great interest to scholars of many disciplines, relating as it does to the history of exploration, science, empire and collecting, Pacific anthropology and British social history of the late eighteenth century. Furthermore, this image was reproduced as a mezzotint from an engraving by John Raphael Smith and published by London printer Molteno Colnaghi & Co. in May 1788. Several copies of these prints exist in museum collections across the world, including New Zealand, Australia and the United States.

An art historian might encounter this painting through a study of late eighteenth-century portraiture or West's work in particular. As an artist working on both sides of the Atlantic and the second president of the Royal Academy in London, he was influential and prolific, and painted many of the leading figures of the day. When considering research questions and primary sources, an art historian's broad research question might be to reveal what this particular piece represents in the development of

2.2 Benjamin West, *Joseph Banks* (1773), England, oil on canvas,
H: 234 cm, W: 160 cm. LCNUG: 1989/9. The Collection: Art and
Archaeology in Lincolnshire, Usher Gallery, Lincoln.

the artist's body of work. In order to do this, they would look to this painting to analyse the artistic technique; the formal elements of the work including tone, line and use of colour; the composition, including the pose of the figure, and its effects; the modelling of the figure; and the handling of the paint. They would look at other portraits to see if particular elements have been borrowed from other paintings, which would offer further insights into West's style of working. They would consider all the objects and clothing depicted in order to dig deeper into the symbolism of the painting as a whole. They might also make qualitative judgements about the work. Stepping back from the painting itself, they would establish the patronage and commission as a means of assessing the world in which West was working, the influences upon him, and his training and background, as well as how this work influenced contemporaries and later artists.

A historian interested in political, imperial and cultural history might choose the same work to interrogate different questions. They should, however, remain attentive to the art historical interpretation. Let us consider how a historian more interested in eighteenth-century elite society (i.e. in Banks, the sitter, rather than West, the artist) would use this portrait. The relationship between the two figures is significant and the commissioning process remains important. Did Banks commission it or did one of the institutions with which he was associated (such as the Royal Society)? How well established was West at the time of the painting; how does his status at the time reflect the meaning of the portrait? Was it a gift? If so, what are the implications of this? How much did it cost? What did such a portrait represent as cultural capital at this time? Display is also important (again returning to possible links to the institutions with which Banks was connected); was the portrait for public or private display? If we want to know about Banks the man and his self-fashioning, how does it compare with other images of Banks? How did the way in which portraitists chose to represent him change over his lifetime? How does this reflect wider changes in society and his role within it? How does the fact that the painting was made into an engraving help us to understand wider society? Enquiring into the creation of the engraving and its dissemination would help us answer this broader question about Banks's influence and role in eighteenth-century society. Applying all of these questions to the painting would enrich a study of Banks the man and, crucially, ensure that the painting is interrogated thoroughly as a source rather than simply as an illustration.

The discussions above, although related to Banks, could in fact be applied to how historians can use portraits more generally. However, this image of Banks (like others in this tradition of portrait painting) has huge potential for historians of collecting, imperial encounters and exploration due to the presence of numerous identifiable objects within it. Banks was one of the first collectors to bring material from the Pacific to Britain and these specific objects, not just generic examples, were part of his collection, much of which is now in the British Museum. Research questions from this perspective therefore have a different angle, and the portrait would fit into a wider project involving other objects and sources:

- How did the production and dissemination of knowledge about the Pacific change during the age of exploration?
- How did exploration and encounter contribute to the formation of British and imperial identity?

These questions could be investigated through a comparison of the objects themselves with their depiction in the portrait: how closely did West observe them? Was ethnographic accuracy important to him or was composition a priority? Did the artist alter elements in the studio (e.g. colour, scale) to fit better with his overall scheme? For these questions relating to exploration and empire, reference to art historical literature would still be helpful, as understanding contemporary conventions would enable the historian to establish the relative significance of the inclusion of material regarded at the time as 'exotic'.

This example serves to demonstrate how different scholars can build up their overarching research questions from an analysis of the object itself. One way to begin to shape these questions is to think about the object or group of objects in question through different lenses. By doing so, you will apply a series of perspectives to the material culture, a strategy that can help you to reveal unforeseen but important research questions.

* This painting, created between 1771 and 1773, is now in the Usher Gallery in Lincolnshire. Helmut von Erffa and Allen Staley, *The Paintings of Benjamin West* (London: The Barra Foundation and Yale University Press, 1986), p. 487, no. 586.

DEVELOPING NEW PERSPECTIVES

When you are planning a new research project, it is most likely that the chosen subject matter is one that has already received some scholarly attention. As such, it is important to find an original approach to this subject. Here, five key issues are presented: value, context, scale, absence and networks. By carefully considering your project in relation to each of these issues you can hone your ideas and check that your research questions and project plan are capable of making a contribution to the field.

Value

As we saw in Chapter 1, the question of value has been central to the study of material culture – in particular, the differences between the financial and social values of objects. While the word 'value' does not always appear within a research question, the majority of studies of material culture do relate in some way to questions of value.[3] There are many different kinds of value to be considered, from emotional to financial, and it is usually important to consider the individual or group who value a particular artefact and how this might change according to chronological, geographical or social context. The biography of the object can affect its value to the owner or collector: 'this was my great-grandfather's watch', 'this was a gift from the Emperor', 'I had this in my bedroom as a child' and so on. 'Values' (in the plural) refers instead to a set of beliefs accepted by an individual or group about what is important to their society. A good understanding of contemporary societal values underpins projects which use objects to examine identity-formation and self-fashioning. It is also often the case that the *value* of an object betrays wider societal *values*. When considering value, it can be helpful to ask yourself *what mattered* to a group of people and to break down your answer into different categories, thereby dividing your larger research question into manageable sections.

An example which vividly demonstrates the range of ways we can consider the value of objects is the porcelain cup depicted in Andrea Mantegna's *Adoration of the Magi* (from the late 1490s; Figure 2.3) recently displayed at the British Museum's Ming: 50 Years that Changed China.[4] In the context of the biblical story it is clear that the Chinese

2.3 Andrea Mantegna, *Adoration of the Magi* (c. 1495–1505), Italy, distemper on linen, W: 48.6 cm, H: 65.6 cm. 85.PA.417. The J. Paul Getty Museum, digital image courtesy of the Getty's Open Content Program.

porcelain cup offered to Christ by the elder Magi was perceived as rare and valuable. In the fifteenth century, when the painting was produced, such wares were highly prized in European courts. Only in the sixteenth century did Chinese export ceramics become more widely available through direct trade between China and Europe. In this painting, as Caroline Campbell informs us, the cup represents the exotic origins of the Magi in the East.[5] Research into the reception and use of Chinese exportware in Renaissance Europe is a vibrant field and Mantegna's painting can offer vital evidence of porcelain's status and meanings, alongside other sources such as inventories and wills. Similarly, the presence of a Persian carpet in the painting offers useful evidence of cultural exchange through trade at this time. Mantegna's painting can be analysed, therefore, as a representation of the value of global things in the late fifteenth century.

If, however, we take a closer look at the likely origins of the porcelain cup – which may have been modelled on one produced in the Jingdezhen region of China – then we encounter other value systems. Jingdezhen porcelain was mass-produced and available in China not only to the elites but also to a much wider social spectrum including the merchants who conducted the porcelain trade. In this light the image of the porcelain cup might prompt a different set of research questions, focused instead upon the original production of such wares and their use in China or other non-European settings. With this approach, the painting is not the most helpful primary source and it would be more useful to examine archaeological finds from the Indian Ocean world alongside trade reports to illuminate the meanings of Chinese porcelain in these alternative cultural contexts. In this way, studying a depiction of an object in a work of art first leads the researcher to the artefact's cultural associations within the world of the painting and its painter, but it can also help you to think beyond these parameters. A single object had great significance within the painting, but such objects embodied different values within the trading context.

In considering questions of the relative value and rarity of particular objects in different social or cultural contexts, we might also think about how this has changed over time, as objects have been added to museum collections. Museums act upon the objects they keep while still providing vital information on objects' meanings in their original context. When an object is transferred to a museum collection, it becomes subject to a new set of meanings which can be revealed in the decision to acquire it, and in its categorisation, storage and display, if it is exhibited.[6] We must be careful not to over-privilege these remnants, as their status as museum artefacts in the twenty-first century does not necessarily reflect their value within original contexts. Take for example a leather shoe in the Amsterdam Museum (inv.nr. DA-35) dated AD 1275–99. This is a rare and exciting find for archaeologists and historians given its composition of easily biodegradable materials and the excellent condition of its preservation. Although it is remarkable that a shoe has survived for 700 years, the shoe was simply footwear to its owner. Close examination of the materials and style of manufacture offers important leads for understanding the lives of ordinary people, but we need other sources to establish the relative value and meaning of such an object.

One skill that art historians or museum curators can contribute to the assessment of value is knowledge about questions of precedence, quality of workmanship and originality. This is not just a subjective aesthetic judgement of quality but also a recognition of the internal history of that kind of artefact. An object has a place in the study of its type as well as in illuminating its historical context. An expert on clocks will say different things about a clock from someone interested in concepts of synchronicity or chronology. It may be a very routine, common, cheap clock or a particularly precious and innovative instrument, but you need to look into the specific study of clocks in order to make this judgement.

The question of value is endemic in the study of material culture, so when you are planning your own project it is worth giving careful consideration to how your sources and argument negotiate this concept.

Context

Objects have long histories. Not only were they involved in multiple contexts during their original creation and use but, when considering objects in museums, their survival to the present day means that they have existed within myriad other historical contexts, all of which might be explored by the historian. When devising a research project, it is important to think about which contexts are most pertinent to answering your research questions: the context of the object's production, its use within the society that produced it or its appropriation by another society or culture. Depending on the objects of study, there may be very many or very few relevant contexts to consider. For example, Roman coins are found across Europe and North Africa – but their discovery in large quantities at the Pudokottai site in South India opens up questions about trade between the Mediterranean and Indian Ocean worlds in the classical era. If you are undertaking an 'object biography' as discussed in Chapter 1, the focus is upon tracing these different contexts and the objects' movement through them. You may, however, focus on one context (i.e. geographical region or period) depending upon your interest or expertise and the questions you are asking.

The study of collecting and the history of exhibitions are perhaps the areas in which the changing context of the object is most important.[7] This rich field investigates the ways in which material culture is acquired and the processes by which objects are removed from one context (which may or may not be its 'original' one) as a gift, through looting or as a purchase, with the purpose of amassing a range of material to form a collection. The nature of the collection could be a personal one, driven by aesthetic preference and the identity of the collector, or the aim might be to assemble objects representative of a culture or geographical place. In this way, histories of collecting connect very closely with ideas both of context and value.

Scale

Determining the scale of your study is a vital consideration in the development of research questions. In the case of material culture this can pertain particularly to the quantity of things that are available to study and the amount of time you have at your disposal. This is where rigorously developing the research questions assists with methodological planning: how many objects and examples are needed to make the case? If the singularity of the object is the reason for its study, this can be reflected in the research questions. Indeed, a question can directly relate to the methodology itself and the process of demonstrating its value. Similarly, consider how many other objects are needed to make the case. Proposing a very wide-ranging study involving objects in multiple repositories is unlikely to be feasible and may undermine your project. By thinking through your methodology and how you will examine the material, you can assess what scope is reasonable and articulate the research questions accordingly.

If undertaking an 'object biography' the focus is often upon a single object over the duration of its existence. This approach could involve research into a much wider range of objects, for example by examining the single object's significance in relation to other relevant objects – similar or different. An object biography would also require contextualisation, potentially within many historical periods and locations. In this case, research questions would reflect how this longitudinal study of a single thing has the potential to unlock an alternative set of insights.

The scope of the project, the questions asked, personal interest and the available material will determine the most appropriate scale. Object-centred studies may tend towards the micro-historical but it is critical that research questions reflect the wider relevance of such focused projects, so take time to step back and highlight the significance of the study and application of its conclusions. An important example of a book-length study that focuses closely on individual objects while still developing larger historical narratives is Laurel Thatcher Ulrich's *The Age of Homespun: Objects and stories in the creation of an American myth*.[8]

Using a combination of material and textual sources, Thatcher Ulrich shows that by examining simple, domestic objects it is possible to develop new interpretations of large cultural, economic and political themes in American society. This is a substantial study, the result of many years of research and writing. However, Thatcher Ulrich's work provides a good example of the ways in which historical material culture studies can move between the micro and the macro, making the findings from individual object studies matter on a larger scale.

Absence

Many historical studies of material things rely entirely on descriptions of material culture when no actual examples of the object remain. The material qualities of the object might mean it no longer survives. The role of collectors in shaping and altering object biographies also needs to be considered. Collectors are selective. Even when personal aesthetic taste is not the primary motivation, no selection of objects can ever claim to be fully comprehensive or culturally neutral. In the early days of the discipline of anthropology, collectors were encouraged to amass material as widely as possible to represent an indigenous culture. However, today these collections are not considered adequate representations of that culture but have come, instead, to be studied as evidence of what one collector could acquire at that time with the help of their networks. These collections are also resonant of assumptions influencing the collector, such as colonial ideologies and ideas about race. Not all kinds of object are considered appropriate for collection – perhaps for political or spiritual reasons.

These complications of available evidence should not prevent us from taking a material-culture-driven approach; and in many cases the absences of the objects are themselves instructive, telling us part of the story. A good example of an informative absence concerns British pre-Reformation Catholic objects, which are rare survivals in the historical record because of the comprehensive efforts to destroy such artefacts during that period of religious and political upheaval. It is important to consider how these absences of evidence will impinge upon the research questions and affect which other primary sources are required. For example, do not set up research questions that would require examination and comparison of original objects if they are not available to you. Ideally your corpus of objects should be accessible for first-hand study; for example, it is not advisable to rely solely on images on a website. Instead, think about adjusting either the research questions or the primary sources you use to develop a robust research project. We will return to the topic of absence in more detail in Chapter 3.

Networks

When planning research, it is helpful to think through the relational aspects of objects both to other objects and to people. The Actor Network Theory (ANT) devised and promoted by Bruno Latour and others provides a useful framework for thinking about relationships, particularly because this theory incorporates objects as equal agents (with humans) within social networks.[9] How do objects bring new relationships between people and cultures into focus? Do these relationships rely on personal contact between objects or between people and objects? In the field of global history, such a focus on networks is particularly relevant as researchers seek to illuminate complex patterns of connections across the world.[10] In a project investigating The Relational Museum, curators at the Pitt Rivers Museum applied network theory to map the connections between individuals, objects and institutions across the world using the Pitt Rivers collection as a starting point. Through this network-centred approach, they interrogated the movement of objects and knowledge in the late nineteenth and early twentieth centuries.[11] Surprising, revealing and hitherto unknown histories emerge from these investigations, ones that inform a wide range of historical disciplines.

Case study:
starting with an object

Colonial rule in Nigeria

A pair of doors from West Africa, measuring 4 m high and 1.5 m wide taken together, hangs in the corner of the Sainsbury Africa galleries of the British Museum (Figure 2.4). They are amongst the largest objects in the gallery and have an imposing physical presence. In depth, the carvings measure 30 cm. These high-relief figures arranged in four registers vividly depict the encounter of two groups – the figures on each level facing towards each other. Closer examination reveals that

2.4 Olowe of Ise, Palace doors of the Ogoga of Ikere (c. 1900), carved and painted wood. Right: Af1979,01.4546.a, H: 230 cm, W: 81.5 cm, D: 20.5 cm; left: Af1979,01.4546.b, H: 220 cm, W: 75 cm, D: 20 cm; lintel: Af1979,01.4546.c. H: 127 cm; W: 46 cm; D: 20 cm. © The Trustees of the British Museum.

the left-hand door represents an African dignitary, seated on a throne, whilst all the other figures are standing. On the right-hand door – on the same register as the leader on the left – is a white figure carried in a kind of hammock by black servants.

Without considering the context in which this object was created, some immediate questions present themselves: Who sculpted it, when and where? Where would the doors have been located? Who are the figures? Was this an actual historical event or an imagined or idealised scene? The dress of the figures (the white figure wearing a pith helmet – a lightweight sun helmet commonly used by Europeans in tropical climates) and the survival of such a large piece of art from this region provide clues as to its context in a colonial society. These are the kinds of questions and answers that can be explored through an encounter with the object itself, but recourse to other sources is revealing of contextual information that can help make sense of the material presentation.

In brief, these remarkable doors depict in high-relief sculptural style the meeting between the Ogoga – political and spiritual leader of the Ekiti people of Ikere – and a British District Officer collecting taxes and dispensing justice in the early twentieth century (in the system known as 'indirect rule'). They were carved by the renowned Yoruba sculptor Olowe of Ise, and came to the British Museum after display at the British Empire Exhibition at Wembley in 1924–5, acquired from the Ogoga following protracted negotiations. They are therefore a vital source for understanding the Yoruba view of colonial governance, a perspective that is largely absent from the documentary record of British administration of the empire.

These doors therefore offer many possible angles for research depending on the skills and interests of the researcher. Questions such as these can provide a good starting point:

- How did the Yoruba perceive and react to the colonial encounter and in what ways did sculpture provide a means to resist and control it?
- What role did political performance play in indirect rule in colonial Nigeria?
- How has the European been depicted in West African sculpture in the pre-colonial period and how did this shift in the colonial era?
- What image of the Yoruba and other West African states was presented in early twentieth-century Britain? How was it received?

Case study:
starting with a period and theme

Private devotion in early modern Europe

Overturning previous assumptions is central to developing historical understanding. The study of religious practice during the Renaissance is well-worn terrain. However, studies to date have primarily focused on the church, the monastery and nunnery, or the religious guilds as sites of religious practice. These are of course essential locations to study, although a focus on the institutions of the church naturally leads to a history that emphasises the role of organised religion in the culture of religious practice. Far less is known, for example, about private devotional practice in the home, and study of this space reveals a very different range of objects and devotional practices from those of church or monastery. A rich vein of scholarship 'looks through the keyhole' to consider private devotion in early modern Europe.[12] Personal Bibles, small majolica Madonnas and rosaries were amongst the most popular kinds of objects venerated within the home. However, as objects of everyday life and of no great artistic status, such things do not survive in great numbers and can sometimes only be studied via mention of their existence in inventories and wills. Religious paintings are other such domestic objects than can help us to understand the ways in which early modern Europeans practised their religions at home. However, the modest nature of such artworks has excluded them from the majority of art historical studies of Renaissance painting and they, therefore, remain a largely unexplored source material. Yet they were some of the most accessible and meaningful devotional items owned by ordinary men and women in the Renaissance period. This subject of study prompts a range of research questions. A wide-ranging question might be:

• How does a focus upon private religious practice transform our understanding of religion in the early modern period?

However, this larger enquiry might be investigated through the following more focused questions:

- What sources can throw light on private behaviour?
- How and where did people pray in the home?
- Which religious books did private individuals read?
- How was religious significance conferred on everyday material objects?
- Were there gender distinctions in family worship?

Case study:
starting with a person

The cult of Lord Nelson

It is easy to accept without further consideration the attraction of objects relating to famous figures. From religious relics to contemporary auction sales of the belongings of celebrities, their tangible links with esteemed, notable or indeed notorious people

2.5 Loving cup with two handles, with portrait of Horatio Nelson, flanked by trophies with inscriptions including the phrase 'England expects every man to do his duty' and a verse praising Nelson (c. 1820), H: 16 cm, W: 24 cm, D: 13.5 cm. AAA4883. National Maritime Museum, Greenwich, London, Walter Collection.

in the past or present will forever hold a fascination. Vice-Admiral Horatio Nelson was a prominent officer in the Royal Navy, celebrated as a hero in his lifetime and after his death for his inspirational leadership and tactical genius. His death at the Battle of Trafalgar in 1805 during the British defeat of the French and Spanish navies became legendary, cementing his reputation as the ultimate British hero. Objects associated with him became prized as relics including the uniform he wore at the time of his death, now on display at the National Maritime Museum while the bullet which shot him is exhibited at Windsor Castle.[13] At the Naval Exhibition of 1892, no fewer than thirty locks of Nelson's hair were displayed in various places around many exhibitions. Beyond articles directly associated with the man himself, an abundance of memorabilia was created from the more standard porcelain statues to jugs and grandfather clocks. Lord Nelson is a useful example, as objects associated with him have been hugely popular and meaningful from the time of his death until the present day. A vast scholarship surrounds his talent as a naval commander and his critical role in the Napoleonic Wars at sea, and the literature also probes into his colourful personal life.[14] However, in the case of the artefacts that belonged to famous historical figures, historians have tended to relegate mention of such objects to a footnote or a fleeting remark. These things, however, can illuminate complex historical narratives and provide opportunities for novel historical research. Of course, individual items have particular stories to tell, while a wider examination of the cult of Nelson can be considered through the following research questions:

- How were personal and 'celebrity' relics consumed in Victorian Britain?
- How does the cult of Nelson reflect British national identity in the nineteenth and twentieth century?
- What does the cult of Nelson tell us about the importance of the navy in the nineteenth century?
- How significant were 'celebrity' objects in wider patterns of production in Victorian Britain?

Case study:
starting with a concept

Reception: Greek sculpture in nineteenth-century Britain

Studies of the reception of ideas are an important strand of scholarship; interrogating the action of historical actors requires an understanding of how *they* perceived precedents and interacted with the past. Texts, and particularly classical texts, have formed a focus for much study of intellectual history. Objects played a critical role in understandings of the classical past and a burgeoning field examines the reception of classical sculpture, in all its forms, in the mid-nineteenth century. Classical sculpture from around the world had been transported to Great Britain in some quantity from the seventeenth century onwards.[15] The collecting of such items and displays of connoisseurship were important features of the experience of the Grand Tour (when members of the upper echelons of British society, and those who could find sponsors, travelled to Europe and in particular Italy to study the culture of the ancient world and the Renaissance and to experience European society). Much of this material, however, remained in elite hands. It was the creation of museums in the Georgian and Victorian periods, as well as the growth of archaeology and British participation within it, which ensured that sculpture from the Mediterranean could be seen by a wider section of the British public. At this time there was a revival in the creation of casts of antique sculpture, driven by the design reform movement and the emergence of a network of schools of art, each requiring a standardised teaching collection. Examples were displayed in the monumental surroundings of the Crystal Palace at the Great Exhibition of 1851 and later in the South Kensington Museum. Plaster casts were initially used but new reproductive technologies, including gelatine casting, facilitated these developments over the centuries. Research questions that respond to this concept, but which also rely on the study of material culture might include:

- To what extent did domestic objects reflect popular interest in classical design and architecture?
- Was classically inspired design available to people of all classes?

- How did the classical education of the elite affect the taste for antique sculpture?
- What role did the cast-makers play in the visual presentation of classical antiquity in Victorian society?

DEVISING A RESEARCH SCHEDULE

At the outset of a project you will need to think through your research questions (as discussed in this chapter), your methodology (the focus of Chapter 3) and your likely sources (Chapter 4). Once you have given these aspects careful consideration, it is time to develop a research plan, including a detailed list of primary sources, locations and an estimated schedule of work. It is important to scrutinise the plan for feasibility within the given timeframe.

Research schedules often plan for a period at the start of the project dedicated to surveying the secondary literature and locating relevant primary sources. Once you have explored secondary literature on the period and theme and decided upon a methodology (see Chapter 3), then you should plan to examine your primary sources. Chapter 4 gives full details on investigating the holdings in repositories and what to expect when you plan a research trip to museums, galleries and other places where you will find collections of historical material culture. After the primary sources have been located and studied closely, you will then need to allocate time to analyse the material in relation to the secondary literature and create your written or final work. It is useful to build some flexibility in to this schedule; it is possible to experience unexpected delays in gaining access to important material. Equally, do not wait to start the process of writing up even if there are one or two pieces of primary evidence still to look at (e.g. an appointment could not take place before this time). These examples can be inserted or you can revise your argument in light of this new material but, in order to meet your deadlines, ensure you allow enough time for writing up.

IN SUMMARY

Thinking carefully about research questions, rather than just research areas or themes, is challenging. Academic supervisors may ask for re-writes of a research proposal, and encourage you to re-think your argument several times. Discuss your project with informal advisors and colleagues, as their opinions can help you to shape your project and refine your approach. Good research questions anchor your project, enable you to limit the scope of the study, help you to feel in control and provide a way of justifying the range of material you have consulted. Your research questions also help shape the final piece of writing by structuring the lines of enquiry. Ultimately research questions should reflect the originality of the contribution of your study to a particular period and geographical context, and make clear the wider relevance of your project to historians of other areas. Furthermore, as mentioned at the start, research proposals form a major part of the work of historians today, so the ability to plan and articulate research projects which immediately capture readers' attention with their originality and feasibility is a valuable skill to develop.

NOTES

1   N. J. Saunders, *Matters of Conflict: Material culture, memory and the First World War* (London: Routledge, 2004). See also online article 'Material Culture and 20th century war' by Nicholas Saunders and Paul Cornish: www.history.ac.uk/ihr/Focus/War/articles/intro.html   [accessed   9 June 2016].

2   A. Gerritsen and G. Riello, 'Introduction: Writing Material Culture History', in A. Gerritsen and G. Riello (eds), *Writing Material Culture History* (London: Bloomsbury, 2015), pp. 1–14, p. 3.

3   For a useful summary of questions relating to objects and value, see R. Friedel, 'Some Matters of Substance', in Lubar and Kingery, *History from Things*, pp. 45–7.

4   For further discussion of this work see Caroline Campbell, 'East meets West in Mantegna's Adoration of the Magi': http://blog.britishmuseum.org/tag/jacopo-bellini [accessed 21 January 2016]; C. Clunas and J. Harrison-Hall, *Ming: 50 years that changed China* (London: British Museum Press, 2014), p. 292. See also R. Finlay, *The Pilgrim Art: Cultures of porcelain in world history* (Berkeley, CA: University of California Press, 2010); R. E. Mack, *Bazaar to Piazza: Islamic trade and Italian art, 1300–1600* (Berkeley, CA: University of California Press, 2001).

5   Campbell, 'East meets West'.

6   A recent project with Harvard museum collections sought to challenge the distinctions forged by Victorian systems of categorisation in museums to break down the boundaries which have determined the

meaning of objects in collections: L. Thatcher Ulrich et al., *Tangible Things: Making history through objects* (Oxford: Oxford University Press, 2015).

7 For references for collecting and museum history see notes 66–8, p. 41. Useful introductory texts include: Pearce, *On Collecting*; Arthur MacGregor, *Curiosity and Enlightenment: Collectors and collections from the sixteenth to the nineteenth century* (New Haven, CT: Yale University Press, 2007).

8 L. Thatcher Ulrich, *The Age of Homespun: Objects and stories in the creation of an American myth* (New York: Alfred A. Knopf, 2001).

9 Latour, *Reassembling the Social.*

10 G. Adamson and G. Riello, 'Global Objects: Intention and entanglement', in M. Berg (ed.), *Writing the History of the Global* (Oxford: Oxford University Press and the British Academy, 2013), pp. 177–93.

11 C. Gosden and F. Larson, *Knowing Things: Exploring the collections at the Pitt Rivers Museum, 1884–1945* (Oxford: Oxford University Press, 2007).

12 See for example L. Roper, *The Holy Household: Women and morals in Reformation Augsburg* (Oxford: Oxford University Press, 1989); J. Martin and A. Ryrie (eds), *Private and Domestic Devotion in Early Modern Britain* (Farnham: Ashgate, 2012). Domestic Devotions: The Place of Piety in the Italian Renaissance Home, 1400–1600, funded by the European Research Council, a major interdisciplinary project involving historians and art historians at the University of Cambridge, is also exploring these questions: http://domesticdevotions.lib.cam.ac.uk [accessed 20 January 2016].

13 R. Prentice, *The Authentic Nelson* (London: National Maritime Museum, 2005).

14 R. Knight, *The Pursuit of Victory: The life and achievement of Horatio Nelson* (London: Allen Lane, 2005); A. Lambert, *Nelson: Britannia's god of war* (London: Faber and Faber, 2004); E. Vincent, *Nelson: Love and fame* (New Haven, CT; London: Yale University Press, 2003).

15 F. Haskell and N. Penny, *Taste and the Antique: The lure of Classical sculpture 1500–1900* (New Haven, CT: Yale University Press, 1981); A. Yarrington and C. Sicca (eds), *The Lustrous Trade: Material culture and the history of sculpture in England and Italy c.1700–c. 1860* (London: Bloomsbury, 2000); R. Frederiksen and E. Marchand (eds), *Plaster Casts: Making, collecting and displaying from Classical antiquity to the present* (Berlin: De Gruyter, 2010); K. Nichols, *Greece and Rome at the Crystal Palace: Classical sculpture and modern Britain, 1854–1936* (Oxford: Oxford University Press, 2015).

RECOMMENDED FURTHER READING

Barringer, Tim J., and Tom Flynn (eds), *Colonialism and the Object: Empire, material culture and the museum* (London: Routledge, 1998).

Black, Jeremy, and Donald M. MacRaild, *Studying History*, 3rd edn (London: Palgrave Macmillan, 2007).

Gerristen, Anne, and Giorgio Riello, 'Introduction: Writing Material Culture History', in Anne Gerritsen and Giorgio Riello (eds), *Writing Material Culture History* (London: Bloomsbury, 2015), pp. 1–13.

Gunn, Simon, and Lucy Faire (eds), *Research Methods for History* (Edinburgh: Edinburgh University Press, 2011).

Harvey, Karen, 'Introduction', in Karen Harvey (ed.), *History and Material Culture: A student's guide to approaching alternative sources* (London: Routledge, 2009), pp. 1–23.

Jordanova, Ludmilla, *History in Practice*, 2nd edn (London: Bloomsbury, 2006).

Lubar, Steven D., and W. D. Kingery (eds), *History from Things: Essays on material culture* (Washington, DC: Smithsonian Institution Press, 1993).

Tosh, John, *The Pursuit of History: Aims, methods and new directions in the study of history*, 6th edn (London: Routledge, 2015).

⇒ 3 ⇐

DEVELOPING A METHODOLOGY

Researching material culture relies on bringing the business of research theory and practice together. As Christopher Tilley has put it: 'Theory *is* practice and all practice *is* theoretical.'[1] Theory and research practice work in concert to drive a research project to a satisfying conclusion. Describing how theory and practice work together is often discussed in the methodology section of a piece of writing, proposal or application. In essence, the term 'methodology' refers to the system of methods used in the study of a given subject. In describing your methodology, you provide a rationale for the selection of particular methods of analysis and the way in which they work together to answer your chosen research question. To this end, Chapter 2 outlined the ways in which a research project might be focused around a specific question, subject or set of sources. Chapter 4 will move on to discuss the details of locating the objects you need to do your research. But, here, the emphasis will be on the over-arching methodology of your research project, which will guide the research work that you conduct in a museum, library or archive.

Research project: a common structure
1. Project summary (what is this about, what are the research questions and why are they interesting and important?)
2. Background (what has been written about this before and by whom?)
3. Methodology (what, if any, theoretical frameworks are you using? What approach will you take? What methods will you use?)
4. Sources (what will you use and why? Where are they located?)
5. Outcomes (what will be produced at the end of this research project?)

When we think about methodologies, we might also think about the methods of analysis that we employ during our research, whether that is object examination, archival research or oral history interviews. Methods of analysis form one part of the overall methodology of a research project. These terms are often confused: to put it simply, the methodology explains the reasoning behind the decision to use particular methods. In Chapter 5, we will take a closer look at these methods, especially in terms of techniques of object analysis, but here we will focus instead on the larger question of the methodology, which is essentially the rationale for your research practice and the theoretical framework within which you position your work. Within historical work that uses material culture, there is a huge diversity of approach. Some projects will focus very determinedly on what specific artefacts can tell us about the past, whilst others might only be able to access their objects through written descriptions or visual depictions. Many studies use material culture to think through larger historical themes concerned with continuity and change over time, identity or the development of ideas. To make this myriad of practice more understandable, here we have divided the study of material culture into two main sections:

1. studies in which an object, a series of objects or a category of object is/are the main focus of the analysis
2. studies which use material culture to develop new perspectives on historical subjects or themes.

Within these broad categories of practice, there exist a wide range of methodologies for combining evidence and analysis effectively to answer research questions.

In general, curatorial research tends to treat the object as the primary focus, whereas academic historians are more likely to engage in the second kind of research. But as historical material culture studies grows, increasingly historians are seeing objects as a starting point for their research – a valuable source material and a helpful conceptual tool. Of course, exploring a material culture subject which lacks surviving or accessible artefacts is also a common challenge for historians. Dealing with the absence of things is, therefore, an important issue for those of us who are interested in material culture and here we will provide some examples of scholarship that negotiates this hurdle and produces interesting results. For studies that focus very closely on material culture sources, objects can still play an important role in illuminating broader historical questions, themes or contexts. However, as we shall see, the way in which material culture is deployed in different methodologies differs quite considerably.

When you are deciding on your methodology it is important to consider the following issues:

- the *research question* or theme (what do you want to know?)
- the range, quality and quantity of your *primary sources* (what is your evidence and how does it help you to answer your question?)
- *methods* or techniques of analysis (e.g. observation, close reading, numerical)
- the *framework* within which you work (e.g. applying a particular theory to your question or working within a quantitative or qualitative research paradigm).

The *research question* or theme should predict your choices on the other points. For example, if you would like to know about the shopping habits of elite Russians living in nineteenth-century Moscow you will need to identify suitable *source* material. This might include personal accounts of shopping in letters or diaries, the accounts or trade cards of expensive Moscow retailers, fashionable items that were commonly bought in these shops, or advertisements for these goods that were printed in newspapers and magazines. In deciding which of these possible sources you would like to use, you will need to think about what quantity and combination of source material will best answer your question. Will you be able to build your argument by using a large sample of newspaper advertisements alone or would it be better to use a combination of advertisements, diaries and shop accounts? If you are doing any quantitative work, such as calculating from shop accounts the frequency of visits from major Moscow shoppers, how many accounts or years of accounts would be sufficient to make your case? What comparisons (regional/chronological) might help you answer your questions? Likewise, if your argument is based more firmly around the qualitative details of shoppers' thoughts about the shopping experience, can you locate material in diaries with sufficient detail? Do they contain information about the perceived value of commodities and consumer decisions?

When deciding on the source material, it is worth taking into account the *methods* of analysis you will need to use. For example, if you are conducting some quantitative analysis, you may need appropriate software to record the data and then skills of statistical analysis to analyse what you have found.[2] The *framework* should be in your mind from the planning stages of the research. For example, if you are applying feminist theory in your analysis of shopping habits in nineteenth-century Moscow, then you will need to make sure the sources and methods of analysis you have chosen are appropriate for thinking about the subject in this way. Usually, you will be working in a framework that is predominantly qualitative or quantitative or a combination of the two. In any of these cases, the most important issue will be ensuring that you have a robust evidence-base and strategy for analysis, allowing you to draw sound conclusions based on your evidence and within the theoretical parameters you have set yourself.

As Anne Gerritsen and Giorgio Riello have commented: 'there is no single way of engaging with material culture'.[3] Moreover, as things stand, 'there cannot be a unified and universal methodology because of the interdisciplinary nature of "material culture history"'.[4] However, as discussed in Chapter 1, there are long-established disciplinary and interdisciplinary traditions upon which we can draw. Here, we will discuss two main approaches, looking first at studies where objects are the main subject and secondly at research which has found new perspectives through an engagement with material culture. Finally, we will discuss the issue of working on material culture that no longer survives. The following examples of scholarship in the field will show that each of the four elements of a research project – *research question, sources, methods* and *framework* – can be shaped to build a rigorous overall methodology. We will start with some examples of work that treats objects themselves as the primary subject, although all of these studies also draw conclusions about wider historical questions.[5] These examples will also guide you in interrogating the methodology within a piece of writing, a skill which is an essential element of historical practice.

OBJECTS AS SUBJECT

Studies that take an object, object type or group of objects as their subject broadly take two main pathways. The first is to keep the study tightly focused on the object itself or its particular life history, and the second is to use an object or objects to explode a broad range of wider themes. Some studies, like Anne Gerritsen's 'The Global Life of a Soya Bottle', do a combination of these two things. Here, we will discuss the ways in which three historians have dealt with objects as their core subject matter, including examples that focus on a specific object, the proliferation of new kinds of material culture and, finally, a category of object.

A specific object

Anne Gerritsen's 'The Global Life of a Soya Bottle' was delivered as a lecture in December 2014 and provides a brilliant example of a study that focuses on one individual object and uses the evidence it presents to illuminate a whole network of historical narratives.[6] Gerritsen deftly deploys this modest soya bottle's life story to generate historical insights and connections that span the globe. It is a good example of how a tight focus on something small and particular need not limit a study to small conclusions or a confined thematic scope. Quite the opposite: objects often allow the researcher to travel in several different directions, following their multiple meanings, their origin and movements, and their relationships with people, places or technologies.

First, Gerritsen closely examines the object itself. The soya bottle is made of tin-glazed clay and is less than 20 cm tall. The text written across the body tells us that it was once located in Dirk Boer's shop in The Hague and that it contained 'Mandarinzoya' (soya). Gerritsen tells us that she is interested in this bottle's 'global story, which speaks to the dynamic cultural exchange between Asia and Europe' in the nineteenth century.[7] But Gerritsen is also interested in this one bottle's 'life story … from its manufactory in Delft to Dirk Boer's shop in the Hague, and its purchase and consumption thereafter'.[8] Gerritsen's analysis of the bottle's material presentation reveals her expertise in ceramics; she quickly establishes that the bottle is made of porcelain and highlights that Europe would probably never have developed this type of ceramic without being prompted by the imports of high-quality ceramics from China. She also comments that the shape of the bottle must have been influenced by Japanese design (based on her specialist knowledge of styles common to both Europe and Japan up until this time). By using the soya bottle as the focal point of the piece, Gerritsen shows that the bottle embodies global histories of technology (the making of porcelain), design and also the fashions in consumption common to northern Europe in the nineteenth century. Moreover, as she follows these connections in material, technique, design, trade and acquisition, the soya bottle becomes a meeting point for much broader trends across many regions of the nineteenth-century world and it shows the interconnectedness, at this time, of different continents and cultures.

As Gerritsen's analysis progresses, she uses the bottle to think about the substance emblazoned across its surface and which it once contained: soya. Of course, in Gerritsen's examination of the bottle she was not able to study its intended contents, which are long gone. Instead she uses a range of other documentary sources – such as poetry, trading company regulations and visual culture – to show that Europeans had encountered soya sauce as early as the 1600s. As she tracks through time, the original soya bottle comes into contact (within her lecture) with other soya bottles sold in Europe between the seventeenth and nineteenth centuries. In this way, for a section of Gerritsen's lecture, the single, specific soya bottle becomes an example of a type of object, a category of thing. The lecture then turns its attention to another feature of the bottle: Dirk Boer's shop, the place in which it was sold. She consults visual images and accounts to consider what other commodities might have been sold alongside soya to answer questions about its relative value in nineteenth-century Dutch society. Connecting objects with the spaces they inhabited is a common technique in historical studies, further contextualising the object but doing so in a way that attends to the material qualities of its environment. Gerritsen therefore uses the bottle not only as her subject but also as a starting point for more than one historical narrative. She uses the physical features of the bottle to guide her research, especially in terms of the explanation of its status in relation to Chinese ceramic technologies and Japanese design styles. However, she does not take her physical examination of the bottle further than that and uses the bottle, instead, to explore broader histories, pulling in documentary or visual sources as needed to develop her narrative and argument.

Gerritsen explains that her approach to the soya bottle has been 'shaped by my own academic trajectories': her training and professional expertise, her colleagues and the institutions she has worked for. This is an important point because Gerritsen is indeed a specialist in ceramics and has skills honed through working directly with museum collections. Other historians working on material culture subjects may not have this training and will, therefore, approach their topic with a perspective that is more likely to be based on close interactions with text rather than artefacts.

Many kinds of object

John Styles's article 'Product Innovation in Early Modern London' is focused on the abundance of new kinds of goods available to ordinary consumers in early modern London and the story this tells us about manufacturing and innovation.[9] For this research, a large range of objects provides the subject of the enquiry and the ramifications of new kinds of interactions between people and things are explored across a series of case studies. Early in his text, Styles comments that, traditionally, historians regarded early modern England as a place with very little material comfort or decoration to offer its lower-status residents. This study makes the opposite argument, suggesting instead that this period saw an unprecedented influx of novel material things that were increasingly accessible to large swathes of the population. This influx took a range of forms: some consumer goods were domestic innovations created to meet the needs of a growing consumer society, some products were designed to substitute foreign imports, and still more were brought from overseas and sold on the British market. However, as Styles notes, new products did not necessarily find new consumers easily and product innovation was a process that was fraught with questions of cost, manufacturing techniques, trade routes, transportation and market place. Styles also emphasises that, whilst the quantitative research on inventories conducted in the 1980s and 1990s has been invaluable in sketching the landscape of early modern material culture, counting the number of objects in people's homes only provides a partial picture.[10] Styles must use different methods to answer his questions about the influx of novel material culture in early modern England. The categories used in quantitative work, such as chairs, beds or mirrors, overlook the diversity that exists within each of these categories. Styles's approach attends, therefore, to the complexities of product innovation and moves beyond macro trends in the numbers and types of goods available to Londoners by paying close attention to 'the physical attributes and individual product histories of the goods concerned'.[11] In this way, Styles employs qualitative analysis alongside quantitative evidence to develop a clearer picture of the social and cultural results of changes in trade and commerce.

The article focuses on London as opposed to other major European cities and concentrates on man-made artefacts rather than consumables such as coffee or tea. The emphasis is on how man-made goods were made ready for the market by manufacturers and dealers. Styles contextualises product innovation in London in terms of the increase in this period in trade between Europe and America and Asia and also the boom in the capital city's population, which rose eight-fold between the mid-sixteenth and mid-eighteenth centuries. It was in these circumstances of population growth and increasing intercontinental trade that London began to manufacture a much broader range of goods, which were capable of competing with foreign imports and which were often designed specifically to do so.

A key case study here is focused on Indian decorated cotton textiles known as 'chintzes', which were imported *en masse* by the East India Company. However, imports of Indian textiles only became widespread (as opposed to a few luxury examples for an elite market) when changes were made to the design. Styles reveals the impact of replacing red grounds with white and relocating the floral decoration to the middle of the textiles. This shift, to meet the preferences of the domestic market, ultimately resulted in patterns developed in England being sent regularly to the manufacturers of the textiles in India, so that the products would closely meet the expectations of English consumers. Through examination of Company correspondence, Styles demonstrates how such a system was flexible enough to respond to changes in fashion at home and, whilst Indian fabrics retained some of their original exotic allure for English consumers, their designs came to have more in common with European than Indian style. This negotiation between the British and the Indian producers is tracked through surviving correspondence of the East India Company and its officials.

Styles's article also explores failed attempts at introducing new products to the English market, a prime example being the East India Company's efforts to sell cotton shifts or shirts in the place of linen ones. Using East India Company records and correspondence, Styles examines the failure of this change in textile to convince the British consumers. Despite offering the product at a much cheaper price than their linen counterparts, concerns about the quality and character of the different materials and workmanship prevailed and the English consumers largely refused this new offering from India. Whilst this example of an adaptation to a traditional garment did not take off, Styles brings to our attention the impressive scale of diversification within early modern material culture through an analysis of Indian textiles, English teapots and branded medical remedies. Achieving a stable, recognisable and desirable product identity was key to success, and manufacturers of branded medicines were early adopters of branded packaging and newspaper advertising in their attempt to sell new products in a crowded market place. Similarly, the sale of ready-made clothing required careful negotiation as eighteenth-century consumers were largely used to buying bespoke garments. In all cases, new products had to incorporate elements of familiarity – in both practical and symbolic terms – in order to be taken up by the English consumers. As Styles comments:

> It was the need to render novelty meaningful and recognizable. The newness of the new product had to be reconciled with consumers' pre-existing experience, knowledge and expectations. Innovation had to be domesticated in almost every sense of that word, from the national to the personal.[12]

In this seminal article on the material culture of early modern London, Styles resists simple narratives focused on the presence of product innovation long before the period of industrialisation or the overwhelming success of these enterprises. Instead he acknowledges the complex push and pull of multiple factors, which, combined, would determine the success, failure or longevity of a particular product. Styles characterises this process as a *negotiation* between supplier and consumer, where expectations were at least partially open to manipulation. Throughout, Styles's argument is augmented with detail concerning the material qualities of particular products and, in this way, he makes a strong case for the need to examine material culture itself in order to understand broader trends in trade, manufacturing and commercial life.

A type of object

Helen Clifford, in her book *Silver in London*, deals with a category of objects, things made of silver, as the subject of her analysis.[13] This work also deals with a material, silver itself, and its social and cultural meanings in early modern England. Clifford's book opens with a compelling description of the importance of silver objects in eighteenth-century London and an acknowledgement that the way we experience these objects today fails to engage the senses or convey the significance of silver things as they were understood in that period.

Objects made from silver and attitudes to them were once central to both economy and society. Today silver is very much back stage and it is difficult for us to imagine its dynamic role in the theatre of social and cultural life. The passive museum objects that sit behind glass, and beyond our reach, do not readily connect with past evocations of the elegance of the tea table and the glamour of the dining room, where silver tea urns and tureens were recognised as active symbols of wealth and status, taste and power.[14]

Clifford's warning about the 'passive' state in which museum objects might appear to us is a prompt to engage closely with objects (and other sources) in order to unlock their dynamism and multiple meanings in society. Silver is the subject of Clifford's enquiry, and surviving silver artefacts provide one of the primary sources for the research. Clifford's object-centred study focuses on a time of change in the manufacture, sale and use of silver: the late eighteenth century. Through this study of production and consumption of silver, she is able to reveal much broader social, economic and cultural developments in London society.

Clifford ensures that 'the silver itself lies at the core of this book', but she also uses documentary sources to help build her narrative of silver manufacture. In particular, Clifford bases much of her analysis on two ledgers – the business accounts of a London manufacturer dating from the 1760s and 1770s. However, throughout, silver objects from museum collections are used as primary evidence and images are supplied.[15] Clifford also makes regular use of visual culture (portraits, conversation pieces, landscapes etc.), trade cards and architectural drawings to build her argument.

The treatment of the material culture of worked silver in Clifford's study attends to both the material and the workmanship that contributed to the value of any silver object. Clifford's detailed examination of both the material qualities of silver and the ways in which it was crafted into tureens, candlesticks and writing paraphernalia is revealing of 'the relative values which a society puts upon silver' and therefore improves our understanding of 'a period and a place, its economy, manners and morals'.[16] By incorporating extant examples of silverware in her study, Clifford is also able to illuminate the reasons why scholarship on silver has traditionally taken certain narrow paths. In particular, she highlights the way in which these expensive and antique silver objects became prominent in the collectors' market of the nineteenth (and subsequently twentieth) century. The exchange of silverware in this context gave it a new set of social and economic meanings, attached very firmly to matters of identification and classification, and the connoisseurial issues of quality of workmanship, rarity of the object and preservation of its form, free from damage or adaptation. The place of silver within the context of this market had led to the discussion of its value in these narrow terms and within a framework which recognised economic value in the here and now over the historical value of silver as evidence of societies in the past. Instead, Clifford's book presents a persuasive argument in favour of a completely different 'reading' of silverware and demonstrates how, by focusing on the material culture and using a wide range of material, documentary and visual sources, silver can illuminate complex human relationships in business, trade, consumer culture, design, fashion, sociability, diplomacy and patronage. In this way, Clifford introduces a new framework within which silver can be studied and reveals the alternative narratives that might be generated by studying silver in its historical contexts.

NEW PERSPECTIVES THROUGH MATERIAL CULTURE

Here we turn to examples of research which explore a historical theme rather than explicitly analysing a form of material culture. It is important that objects are not merely used as illustrations in historical work, and so paying close attention to the kinds of evidence presented by material culture and the potential insights it can offer will still help with the writing of a piece that examines a theme rather than focusing explicitly on objects. Taking a rigorous approach to your selection of primary sources (material culture or otherwise) is always advisable when starting a research project. Through the careful consideration of whether your assumptions about the value of one piece of evidence over another are correct, you might find that new questions or forms of evidence present themselves to you. Here, we will discuss three examples of studies in which material culture acts as a provocation to thought and brings new perspectives to bear upon a particular theme or period. In the first instance, Vivienne Richmond's research shows how an object can act as a starting point for a research question even if the project subsequently develops through an analysis of textual sources. The second study, by Matt Houlbrook, analyses the significance of an object in a particular historical context to gain new perspectives on issues of gender and sexuality. Finally, Sarah Longair's research explores the display of an exhibition as a phenomenon closely related to material things, but which can be studied through a variety of source material. In each case, material culture – physically or conceptually – provides opportunities to develop new perspectives on historical questions.

A specific object

To take an example of a study that uses the evidence of artefacts as a starting (if not an end) point, we have Vivienne Richmond's essay 'Stitching the Self: Eliza Kenniff's Drawers and the Materialization of Identity in Late-Nineteenth-Century London'. The chapter begins as follows:

> Researching the archive of the English Girls' Friendly Society (GFS), a Victorian organization for working-class girls, I chanced upon a late-nineteenth-century plain-sewing needlework sampler and a pair of calico drawers. Both were attributed to E. Kenniff and entered in a GFS exhibition of members' work. My interest in proletarian dress, extant examples of which are rare, meant they immediately caught my attention, but more than this, I wondered, who was E. Kenniff?[17]

3.1 A sketch by Vivienne Richmond of a pair of hand-stitched drawers found in the English Girls' Friendly Society Archive. Reproduced with permission.

Here, Richmond's larger research questions concern the girl or woman who made the needlework objects and the working-class culture that they represented, especially in terms of dress. This chapter has since been re-published in a collection of essays on gender and material culture and in this version of the text, Richmond makes her research process more explicit, walking the reader through the development of her investigation into the sampler and calico drawers.[18]

The key pieces of material evidence used in Richmond's chapter are a pair of prize-winning, hand-stitched drawers (underwear) and a sampler (Figure 3.1).[19] These hand-made items left Richmond with clues as to the identity of their maker or makers: a cross-stitched square reading: 'GFS / S Andrew's Branch / E Kenniff / Age 12' and a note on the sampler revealing that 'E' stood for 'Emily'. The fact that they were prize-winning is likely to be the reason for the unusual retention of clothing such as underwear. Richmond uses census data to search for the maker of the items and, through her use of documentary evidence from the census and the Girls' Friendly Society archive in combination with the material objects themselves she is able to discover that the drawers were, in fact, made by another 'E Kenniff': 'Eliza', Emily's sister. The analysis develops from the small, personal textile artefacts to a discussion of class, gender, dress and propriety in nineteenth-century London. For Richmond, rare textile survivals of Victorian working-class dress are hugely important to her understanding of the social and cultural meanings of working-class clothes. She notes: 'Through this [material culture] they created material autobiographies which left vivid clues about who they were and how they wished to be perceived.'[20] In studying proletarian lives and garments, the latter rarely surviving to be examined by the historian, Richmond has often had to rely on textual sources to explore her subject.[21] However, in this chapter she shows how, when presented with a rare example of such a garment, it is possible to build a more detailed picture of individual working-class women's lives and identities. In other words, the objects unlock precious personal details about individuals who remain obscure in historians' accounts of that period and place.

A symbolic object

Matt Houlbrook's article 'The Man with the Powder Puff in Interwar London' was published in the *Historical Journal* in 2007 and represents an excellent example of a study that focuses on the symbolic meaning of one kind of object (rather than a particular example of that object).[22] In fact, Houlbrook has not relied on the study of powder puffs in order to write this article: he neither includes an image of one nor does he refer to having handled a contemporary example. Nevertheless, the powder puff acts as a powerful actor in his text. In particular, Houlbrook uses the powder puff to explore questions of object agency alongside much broader themes in interwar cultural and crime history.

The research for this article did not begin with the powder puff as an object; instead, Houlbrook was intrigued by a news story in the weekly journal *John Bull*, entitled 'The man with the powder puff' (January 1925), which told readers about a miscarriage of justice. The unfortunate subject was a young man from Wales, who had been arrested on the streets of London for approaching men for 'immoral purposes' or, in other words, for engaging in homosexual activities. The key pieces of evidence for the man's 'deviant character' were 'a lady's powder puff, powder and a small mirror' which were found on his person.[23] In this case, it seemed that the possession by a man, rather than a woman, of these cosmetics marketed to female consumers was enough to convict him of what was at this time an illegal sexual act. As Houlbrook explains: 'According to this logic, the man who owned a powder puff was effeminate; the effeminate man possessed illicit sexual desires; such a man was, in police jargon, of the "male importuning type".'[24] When found in the pockets of a man, an otherwise innocuous commodity became a signifier of transgressive sexual desire. However, *John Bull* had an alternative explanation and was outraged on the young man's behalf that he had been 'branded with the mark of infamy'.[25] The journal stressed that the man only visited London a few times a year and that he was, on this occasion, in town to visit the British Empire Exhibition with his mother – a perfectly respectable activity. The explanation given for the powder puff in his pocket was simply that he had offered to carry it for his mother whose bag had broken. However, as Houlbrook points out, *John Bull* did not question the association that the police had made between the powder puff and male effeminacy, just the legitimacy of their accusing this upstanding young man on a day out with his mother. It is through this odd legal case, taken up by the popular press, that Houlbrook finds cause to dwell on the symbolic resonance assumed by the powder puff in interwar London and its variegated relationships with London streets, sexuality, gender and consumer culture.

Having opened with this particular case and its reporting, Houlbrook contextualises the example by showing that it was not unusual for the police to use the evidence of possession of cosmetics to convict men of 'importuning'. In these circumstances, then, the powder puff took on significant symbolic power, and this and other similar episodes reveal the 'growing salience of the effeminate "painted boy" to public understandings of sexual difference in the 1920s'.[26] The powder puff was used in criminal prosecutions in a very particular way. Unlike other pieces of evidence, it was not itself directly connected to the crime in question. Instead, it was being used to demonstrate that someone was a 'criminal type' rather than to substantiate a particular criminal act.

In the article's analysis, the complex connections between constructions of gender and sexuality are explored in relation to consumer culture and the marketing of commodities for the beauty industry of the period. Criminal cases are also a rich source for material culture historians; they use objects as evidence and reveal societal codes and values. In particular, using evidence from police reports and newspapers, Houlbrook shows how men who sought sexual acts or relationships with other men were characterised as feminine. This elision of sexual attraction to men and the female gender played into the symbolism of women's cosmetics in the prosecution of sexual transgression.

During this period, the beauty industry was gaining momentum as manufacturing techniques facilitated affordable cosmetics and advertising encouraged women to see powder and lipstick as modern necessities, rather than occasional luxuries. Houlbrook uses advertisements and secondary literature about these technological developments to put cosmetics into broader regimes of value. As he argues: 'In reconfiguring the landscape of fashionable femininity, the beauty industry thus simultaneously reconfigured the visual and material signs in which observers – including the police – located queer men's deviance.'[27] Moreover, Houlbrook situates moral panic about sexual transgression within the shifting sands of Britain following the First World War. The social context of this era included the effects of the Great War on British society, the destabilising of gender roles through women's war work, a prevailing concern with upholding traditional standards, and much moral outrage in the press about the 'painted boy menace'. As Houlbrook concludes, thinking in these terms highlights the intersection between discrete historical processes – the emergence of the 'cosmetics industry', a particular understanding of sexual difference, the contentious politics of policing, and worries over the stability of social identities – which made such cases so common after the First World War.[28] But whilst the possession of a powder puff by a man could be deployed as clear evidence of his transgressive nature, this was by no means a stable meaning. Cosmetics, owned or worn by men or women at this time, might have a range of meanings. However, in each instance objects could have agency and an ability to act upon people's lives; an object entirely neutral in the hands of a woman acquired a criminal meaning when discovered by the police in the pockets of a man. The use of powder puffs by the police provides an example of attempts by law enforcement to clearly delineate gendered normality from deviance and to control these boundaries. The powder puff, as a newly prevalent commodity of the era, played an important role in the contested spaces of gender identity and sexual desire.

An exhibition as subject

Sarah Longair's article '"A Grand Show" for East Africa: The Zanzibar Exhibition of 1905' explores as its subject an exhibition of objects presented in Zanzibar at the beginning of the twentieth century.[29] The exhibition was 'explicitly designed to promote trade and commerce' in the archipelago located off the coast of East Africa and was 'conducted with the pomp and splendour characteristic of the frequent ceremonies of Zanzibar's British and Omani Arab elites'.[30] As such, the article uses an instance of an exhibition of objects to explore the broader theme of colonialism in the social, economic and cultural context of an imperial territory on the periphery of the British Empire. By focusing on an exhibition, Longair is able to examine the construction of the image of Zanzibar as a valuable region to the empire through the display of objects associated with art and industry, tradition and modernity, but also the tensions within this image of the Protectorate.[31] Although this article is about objects in the sense that, together, they compose an exhibition, material culture is not its primary subject matter. Instead, the article uses a range of visual and documentary sources to discuss questions of colonialism and East African history, accessing objects as evidence through the photographic and textual record of the event itself. In particular, the photograph albums of Alexander Stuart Rogers, the British first minister who oversaw the exhibition, are mined for what they reveal of the objects and their arrangement within the exhibition, alongside official documents and reports published in newspapers in Zanzibar and East Africa. Longair contextualises the Zanzibar exhibition with reference to other trade and industry exhibitions which made their mark on the world stage, not least the 1851 Great Exhibition in London, and illuminates these events as 'cultural tools of empire'.[32]

The article considers in detail the different selections of objects to exhibit and the juxtapositions imposed within the exhibition's design. Some displays focused on the natural products of Zanzibar, promoting the territory as fertile and profitable, whilst others emphasised the cultural life of the islands. However, material culture was put in the service of the imperial project, ensuring that existing power relationships were upheld. In particular, the placement of Swahili regalia alongside other objects and trophies in a special display of Rogers's personal collection created a hierarchy which reduced Zanzibari objects to the status of curios. Overall, this study provides a good example of the insights provided by histories of collecting and exhibiting applied to a particular colonial context at the beginning of the twentieth century. In this case the objects themselves provide valuable supporting evidence of the kinds of product that were considered important to – or emblematic of – Zanzibar in this period, but it is their arrangement within the larger exhibition and the intentions behind this international event that provide the thrust of the narrative.

DEALING WITH ABSENT OBJECTS

It will often be the case that material culture of relevance to your historical enquiry no longer survives in museums or collections. This could be because the material in question is ephemeral or because it was not considered important enough to keep. It might be that only very few examples exist of an artefact that was previously common and that the extant examples are either inaccessible or do not offer enough evidence to answer your questions. Some important objects have, of course, been lost and many historical sites or built heritage have subsequently been demolished or adapted beyond recognition. Our material heritage is, like our other primary sources, partial. However, where material culture does not survive to speak for itself, it is still possible to use objects as both the subject of your research or as the evidence you use to support a broader argument. In these cases, it will be necessary to reconstruct material culture via other primary sources, such as documentary sources, visual culture or literature. Matt Houlbrook's analysis of the significance of the powder puff, for example, did not involve an examination of such an item. Historians of dress, especially of the seventeenth century and earlier, rely heavily upon images, descriptions, manuals and bills to reconstruct how clothing appeared, often with few surviving specimens to examine. Inventories, as noted above, are fruitful sources for historians as they list the possessions of an individual or family home even if the objects no longer exist.[33] Their form and level of detail in describing objects can vary but these sources open up many possibilities for historians. Here, two examples will be used to elucidate the ways in which historians have built strong arguments around material culture without relevant surviving artefacts at their disposal. A last example will look instead at where the material can fill absences that exist within the textual record, especially when they can be rooted in a specific geographical and cultural location.

Absent objects in vanished spaces

In Helen Smith's study entitled 'Gender and Material Culture in Early Modern London Guilds', she makes a case for women's integral involvement with metropolitan guild life in the sixteenth and seventeenth centuries.[34] However, the material evidence of early modern guild halls has largely been destroyed. Instead, Smith had to use textual sources to unlock evidence of the buildings and objects that composed these significant institutions. Her chapter provides a good example of scholarship that focuses on what material culture can tell us about social, cultural economic or political life but does so in the absence of relevant material or architectural sources. Much historical scholarship on material culture falls into this category and it is revealing of the ways in which thinking about material culture, even when that material culture cannot be studied in person, can prompt new interpretations of the past.

Guilds were organisations established by craftsmen who had occupations in common and wished to protect their economic privileges and strengthen the social ties of craft or trade. In early modern London there were twelve important and powerful companies of workers: the Mercers, Grocers, Drapers, Fishmongers, Goldsmiths, Skinners, Merchant Taylors, Haberdashers, Salters, Ironmongers, Vintners and Clothworkers.[35] Essentially, guilds supported the collective objectives of their members, and their buildings and material culture embodied a sense of community and occupational pride. Traditionally, these spaces have been seen as being occupied almost exclusively by men, and the community identities they helped to reinforce as highly masculine in character. In England women were not officially excluded from joining a guild, although very few did so, and Smith's article contributes to a small but growing literature that has uncovered women's participation in the life of the guilds. Of course, many women did work alongside their husbands who were active participants in guilds. Moreover, women who were widowed might run businesses in their own right. So, whilst men made up the vast majority of individuals with membership of a guild, women were not entirely absent from either the work itself or the accompanying community sociability. As Smith highlights, 'the relationships between gender identity and the spaces of urban and civic life, most notably the guildhalls, were complex', shaping and being shaped by behaviours relating to business and social life. The interiors of guildhalls were also adapted over time, parts of them being given over to private residence for senior guild officials or designated for communal, company activities as required.[36]

Smith builds a picture of women's participation in guild life through her analysis of textual sources from the period, especially court minutes and wardens' accounts, but it is the material culture recorded in these documents that provides new evidence of women's activities in these institutions. Women were involved in the construction of halls (as builders, painters and plumbers) and also in their making of decorative objects for these spaces, such as hand-made textiles. Women were also present in these spaces, not only through the objects that they had made, but in the domestic work they regularly carried out – cleaning, washing and polishing pewter.[37] This kind of work has typically been ignored in studies of guild life because of the persistent prejudices that separate 'important', productive labour from domestic work. As Smith emphasises, women's work of all kinds formed part 'of the essential rhythm of operations of the guild and their memberships', supporting the guild in a key function: its 'capacity for the civic and social display of "brotherhood"'.[38] Here, the material culture and buildings no longer exist to be examined by the historian, but Smith makes deft use of textural sources to illuminate the material world of the guild and, in so doing, the much overlooked involvement of women in company life.

An inventory of the disappeared

Nuno Senos deals with an absent collection in his examination of the inventory of the Portuguese Duke of Bragança in which he seeks to explore the Duke's world view through the material he amassed relating to Portugal's maritime empire.[39] The Duke died in 1563, having been head of the most influential family of the Portuguese nobility. At this point his estate was divided between his four heirs. In order to calculate and manage this separation, a vast inventory was made with over 6,000 entries, taking over four years to compile. The aim of his study is not to trace the paths of these objects following the division of the collection. Instead, he uses the inventory to answer questions about global connections and imaginative geographies. He selects a range of objects described in the inventory to demonstrate the challenges of deciphering the terminology of the inventory and then makes references to objects in museum collections to help him identify the kinds of objects to which the inventory entries refer. By using contemporary museum objects whose place of production is known, Senos is able to reveal some of the assumptions the early modern Portuguese elite made about the world they lived in. For example, in the inventory, the term 'India' refers to the region between the Cape of Good Hope and Melaka, and 'China' incorporates all regions east of Melaka. Using museum objects, he is able to be much more specific about the likely source of individual items. Few objects were collected from Brazil, which was not deemed 'collectable' by the Portuguese, perhaps because they did not esteem its material productions. The monetary value assigned to different objects in the inventory illuminates the status placed not only on particular artefacts but also on regions of the world. Due to the historical context, slaves were also included in the inventory and they were by far the most valuable 'commodities' listed.

Senos also uses the inventory to examine where objects might have been located in the Duke's palace, the Vila Viçosa. The inventory is not organised, as some were, by location but by which member of the Duke's staff was responsible for the items in question. However, he is able to make some inferences from the inventory. Senos infers that the quantity of Indian material – over 107 objects from textiles to weapons – suggests that they were located around the palace, furnishings in bedrooms and arms in the armoury. He also turns to other sources to establish objects' locations, in particular the reports provided by visitors to the palace. In these testimonies, Turkish and Persian carpets are regularly noted as being present throughout the palace. Although there are a large number of 'exotic' items – jugs of mother-of-pearl or forks with rock crystal handles – which, at that time, were commonly located in the cabinets of curiosity of elite European households, Senos can find no evidence that the Duke chose to display his collection in this way. It seems that: 'Once a coconut from the Indian Ocean, for instance, was mounted in silver and became a precious work of art, it entered the regular decorative discourse of the palace and became an object to be displayed next to German silver candle holders, on top of a Portuguese table, against the background of a set of Flemish tapestries that tell the story of Alexander.'[40] Foreign objects appear to have ceased to be exotic within the context of the Duke's home. Senos concludes by analysing objects kept in the Duke's personal office, including a number of objects related to maritime enterprise, including maps, globes, compasses, astrolabes, and books on navigation and global travel accounts. Again, he identifies an organisational method that did not emphasise the exotic as much as it showcased knowledge as a global commodity. Through this inventory, in the absence of the objects themselves, Senos begins to reconstruct the material world of the Duke and draw conclusions about how his possessions reveal his relationship to Portuguese maritime expansion.

Location matters

The question of absence can be approached from another angle – that is, by thinking about what objects can reveal that is hidden from the written record. A stimulating example of this can be found in an essay by Ian W. Brown in which he examines 'The New England Cemetery as a Cultural Landscape'.[41] In contrast to museums which divorce objects from their original social and cultural environment, Brown views cemeteries as 'cultural landscapes' where material culture can be viewed in their intended context. This essay traces the burial arrangement of the Coolidge family through six generations. His interest was sparked by the fact that one member, Elizabeth, who died of smallpox in 1776, was buried separately far from the bulk of the Coolidge graves, which were clustered together. He initially assumed that this had been a form of isolation to prevent this feared disease 'contaminating' the rest of the family. Brown breaks with the traditional way in which scholars had hitherto examined cemeteries – that is, by concentrating upon the text on individual gravestones – by stepping back to consider the burial patterns. Brown posits that 'the location of graves in a cemetery reflects to some degree the social relationships of the deceased', and uses the spatial arrangement of graves to reveal emotional relationships often hidden in the historical record.[42]

The Coolidge family used the cemetery for six generations, almost 150 years, allowing patterns to be discerned. Brown further refines the selection of graves to be studied to a group of twenty-six people representing these six generations marked by twenty-two stones, buried between 1680 and 1823. He then maps the graves within the site according to generations (drawn from documentary records of births and deaths) and family-lines to assess how the positioning of one grave had an effect upon the next. This close analysis revealed that one line of the family tended to bury their family in close proximity while another scattered theirs over a larger area. Elizabeth Coolidge was part of the line of the family who consistently buried their dead widely across the cemetery and therefore her disease cannot be seen as the reason for the placement of her grave. Brown infers that one line of the family appeared to have maintained closer social relations than the other line. While he relied upon written sources to reconstruct the genealogies, he notes that '[t]he relative positions of the death provide a view of relationships that one would never be able to appreciate by studying genealogies alone'.[43] He concludes by emphasising the importance of location and locating objects in space to enhance our understanding of the past: 'It is the context, including the control of time, space, and form, which provides the power generated in material culture research. Without context our contributions to history are indeed minimal, but with it we can view the people of the past in ways that could never have been anticipated by students of the written record.'[44] This idea of cultural landscapes is a powerful concept which demonstrates clearly how objects in context fill absences in history written solely using written sources.

IN SUMMARY

In the examples explored here, a wide range of methodologies is evident. These examples of contemporary scholarship have very different starting points and directions of travel, but they have all had to make careful decisions about the way in which range and type of primary source and modes of analysis are capable of answering defined research questions. In the next chapter we will look in more detail at the places where material culture can be located and the ways in which researchers can gain access to this important source material.

NOTES

1 C. Tilley (ed.), *Reading Material Culture: Structuralism, hermeneutics and post-structuralism* (Oxford: Basil Blackwell, 1991), p. vii.

2 For a guide to doing quantitative history and statistical analysis, see P. Hudson, *History by Numbers: An introduction to quantitative approaches* (London: Arnold, 2000) and L. Haskins and K. Jeffrey, *Understanding Quantitative History* (Cambridge, MA: MIT Press, 1990).

3 Gerritsen and Riello, *Writing Material Culture History*, p. 5.

4 Ibid.

5 This relates to asking the 'so what' question of your planned project, as discussed in Chapter 2, p. 48.

6 A. Gerritsen, 'The Global Life of a Soya Bottle', an inaugural lecture at the University of Leiden, 12 December 2014, see https://openaccess.leidenuniv.nl/handle/1887/32170 [accessed 10 September 2016].

7 Ibid., p. 3.

8 Ibid.

9 J. Styles, 'Product Innovation in Early Modern London', *Past & Present*, 168 (2000), 124–69.

10 Excellent examples of this kind of foundational work on material culture include Weatherill, *Consumer Behaviour and Material Culture*, P. Earle, *The Making of the English Middle Class: Business, society and family life in London, 1660–1730* (London: Methuen, 1989); Shammas, *Pre-Industrial Consumer*.

11 Styles, 'Product Innovation', 126.

12 Ibid., 165.

13 For another example of a study focused entirely around one material (and the objects that are made from it), see G. Riello, *Cotton: The fabric that made the modern world* (Cambridge: Cambridge University Press, 2013).

14 H. Clifford, *Silver in London: The Parker and Wakelin partnership, 1760–1776* (London: Yale University Press, 2012), p. 2.

15 Clifford uses objects from a wide range of collections, including: the Ashmolean Museum, Oxford; Museum of Fine Arts, Boston; the

British Museum; Brasenose College, Oxford; The Lord Mayor and Corporation of Bristol; the Bill Brown Collection, Worshipful Company of Goldsmiths; Leeds City Art Galleries, Temple Newsam House; Kenwood House, London; the Victoria & Albert Museum, London; Sir John Soane's Museum, London; the National Trust, Anglesey Abbey; the Gilbert Collection Trust, London; The Hyde Collection, Harvard University; the Royal Naval Museum, Portsmouth; The Royal Academy, London; Oriel College, Oxford; and also from antiques dealers and private collections.

16 Clifford, *Silver in London*, p. 3.

17 V. Richmond, 'Stitching the Self: Eliza Kenniff's drawers and the materialization of identity in late-nineteenth-century London', in M. Goggin and B. Fowkes Tobin (eds), *Women and Things: Gendered material strategies, 1750–1950* (Farnham: Ashgate, 2009), pp. 43–54.

18 See V. Richmond, 'Stitching Women: Unpicking histories of Victorian clothes', in H. Greig, J. Hamlett and L. Hannan (eds), *Gender and Material Culture in Britain since 1600* (London: Palgrave, 2015), pp. 90–103.

19 For more information on drawing as a method of recording objects of study, see Chapter 5, pp. 127–8.

20 Richmond, 'Stitching the Self', p. 52.

21 For more on primary sources in dress history see I. Mida and A. Kim, *The Dress Detective: A practical guide to object-based research in fashion* (London: Bloomsbury, 2015).

22 M. Houlbrook, 'The Man with the Powder Puff in Interwar London', *Historical Journal*, 50:1 (2007), 145–71. This article was re-published in Greig, Hamlett and Hannan (eds), *Gender and Material Culture*, pp. 120–37.

23 Houlbrook, 'The Man with the Powder Puff', 146.

24 Ibid.

25 Ibid.

26 Ibid., 148.

27 Ibid., 158.

28 Ibid., 170.

29 S. Longair, '"A Grand Show" for East Africa: The Zanzibar Exhibition of 1905', *exPLUSultra*, 3 (2012), 1–19.

30 Ibid., 1–2.

31 Ibid., 2.

32 Ibid., 3.

33 For general texts on the use of inventories in the early modern period, see J. Keating and L. Markey, 'Introduction: Captured Objects: Inventories

of early modern collections', *Journal of the History of Collections*, 23:2 (2011), 209–13; G. Riello, '"Things Seen and Unseen": The material culture of early modern inventories and their representation of domestic interiors', in P. Findlen (ed.), *Early Modern Things: Objects and their histories, 1500–1800* (London: Routledge, 2013), pp. 125–50.

34 H. Smith, 'Gender and Material Culture in the Early Modern London Guilds', in Greig, Hamlett and Hannan (eds), *Gender and Material Culture*, pp. 16–31.

35 Ibid., p. 17.

36 Ibid., pp. 19–20.

37 Ibid., p. 26.

38 Ibid.

39 N. Senos, 'The Empire in the Duke's Palace: Global material culture in sixteenth-century Portugal', in Gerritsen and Riello (eds), *Global Lives of Things*, pp. 128–44.

40 Ibid., p. 139.

41 I.W. Brown, 'The New England Cemetery as a Cultural Landscape', in Lubar and Kingery (eds), *History from Things*, pp. 140–59.

42 Ibid., p. 146.

43 Ibid., p. 156.

44 Ibid., p. 158.

RECOMMENDED FURTHER READING

Findlen, Paula (ed.), *Early Modern Things: Objects and their histories, 1500–1800* (London: Routledge, 2013).

Hudson, Pat, *History by Numbers: An introduction to quantitative approaches* (London: Arnold, 2000).

Lubar, Steven D. and W.D. Kingery (eds), *History from Things: Essays on material culture* (Washington, DC: Smithsonian Institution Press, 1993).

Mida, Ingrid, and Alexandra Kim, *The Dress Detective: A practical guide to object-based research in fashion* (London: Bloomsbury, 2015).

Weatherill, Lorna, *Consumer Behaviour and Material Culture in Britain, 1660–1760* (London: Economic and Social Research Council, 1985).

4

LOCATING SOURCES: UNDERSTANDING MUSEUM COLLECTIONS AND OTHER REPOSITORIES

Objects surround us at all times. You may decide to study material that is not housed in object-based institutions, such as personal objects acquired through friends or family. In these cases you will already know of the object's existence and where to find it. However, for many researchers with an interest in history, objects of study will be found within a cultural institution such as a museum, gallery or heritage site. Even if your primary sources lie elsewhere, it may be helpful to use museums and heritage sites to locate comparable examples of the objects in question. A significant portion of this chapter therefore discusses museums and heritage sites as these offer the most readily available sources of material culture for scholars, and offers detailed guidance on searching collections and forging good relationships with institutional staff, whose expertise will be critical. Using collections located in such institutions has many advantages: accessible information about their holdings on websites (and in some cases online databases) and existing research on the collection upon which to build new findings. These collections are also stored in secure facilities in a stable condition. However, institutions of this kind are only the most well-known repositories of objects. Many other kinds of organisation retain historical records – and sometimes material things – including hospitals, schools, societies, department stores or manufacturers. Beyond public and private institutions, individuals may also hold collections of artefacts of interest to the historian. Whilst institutions have their own procedures and priorities, arranging to research privately held material in personal collections has its own demands and ethical issues which require care and tact.

It is likely that in preparing research questions and developing a methodology, you will have a good sense of the core material to be examined and may well have already seen examples of it. Indeed, developing a research question without confirming that the material is accessible to you can waste time and jeopardise relations with either an institution or an individual. This chapter will provide practical guidance on accessing museum collections and other repositories of material culture necessary for developing your research project and locating your sources. Understanding the ways in which object-based institutions organise their collections is essential to finding your primary sources and understanding the absences that exist in the historical record. While there are common standards and forms of documentation, every institution has their own system that needs to be understood in order to be navigated. Explaining how you came to terms with the different archival structures surrounding material collections will often form part of your final written piece when you discuss your sources (see Chapter 6, pp. 145–8). For historians, the documentation that relates to chosen objects may also be very useful and this can either be found with the object or in a number of different locations within the same institution or elsewhere.

When conducting primary research within institutions and archives, you will be faced with far more material and potential avenues than can be covered within a single research project. During museum visits, objects that did not spring to mind when planning the project might suddenly come to light: for example, when you see two objects in close proximity. Such serendipitous moments can be inspiring and exciting, but must also be documented carefully if you are to make the best use of unforeseen finds. To be effective in the face of new information, record as many details as you can during your research visit and, before proceeding, reflect carefully on whether these additional sources help you to answer your research questions.

On pages 44–6 in Chapter 2, two different scenarios were outlined, showing the main points of entry into a historical study: a) when the period is determined but not the specific primary sources and b) where the primary sources act as a starting point. That section described the different locations where you might be likely to find material. It is also worth highlighting that it can be challenging to establish which museums contain the material you seek. If you are unsuccessful in your initial searches through the most obvious institutions, there are other routes. For example, archaeological material found by the public in the UK is added to the Portable Antiquities Scheme database (www.finds.org.

uk/database – accessed 26 May 2016). Other archaeological databases – such as Historic Environments Records – can also help to find material from historic and archaeological sites administered in the UK at county level (www.heritagegateway.org.uk/gateway/chr – accessed 26 May 2016).

Early on in your project, it is advisable to keep a detailed record of all the objects and collections you may wish to consult. It might be that you are only able to visit a small number of these in person, but it is important to retain all the records you make about objects in inaccessible collections as well as those you can visit, as the quantity you chose to focus upon, and the reasons for this selection (whether intellectual or practical), should be discussed in the methodology section of your final written work. Keeping systematic notes (for example in a spreadsheet or detailed list) enables you to create your own 'database' of objects relevant for the study and will be invaluable when you come to analyse your findings.

Digital resources relating to material culture take many forms: most obviously databases cataloguing museum objects, some of which contain images which allow you to see the objects you might consult. In addition, there are a host of other digital resources which can help support and enhance research. As with all primary sources, digital objects must be treated with care and it is worth taking time to verify the provenance of films, documents, images and photographs that you wish to use in your research but which you will not be able to examine in person.

This chapter will help you to understand how these different repositories and institutions organise their collections so that you can search them effectively and make the most of all the sources (written and material) within them. First, it will focus on how to navigate institutions with catalogued collections: these repositories are extremely useful for historians as they often have the widest selection of material with known provenance. Such institutions exist for a range of historical reasons and their collections reflect the reasons for their foundation and their history as an institution. Understanding this background will help you gain a picture of the 'anatomy' of the collection and, in turn, elucidate the logic by which that collection has been arranged. As we shall see, using museums for research is different from visiting a library or archive and it is important to consider these differences and plan for them when you are conducting your research. To this end, we will outline how to navigate documentation in institutional collections, so that you can locate the objects you wish to see. One approach is to survey an institution's catalogue before finalising your research questions, but it is equally valid to consult the catalogue after deciding upon your subject and methodology. In either case, understanding the structure and logic of the collection will enhance the research process as you can look critically at the sources available. The chapter will then discuss the procedures for approaching these institutions and the methods by which you gain access to the material. Finally, the chapter considers other locations – aside from museums, galleries and heritage sites – where it might be possible to locate material culture for the purposes of research.

NAVIGATING CATALOGUES AND DOCUMENTATION

The principal functions of a museum, gallery or collecting institution include storing, safeguarding and displaying objects. But these objects mean very little for the organisation without documentation to explain them. To fulfil these core responsibilities, consistent and accurate recording-keeping is fundamental. At a basic level, this can involve specifying what is in the collection and where it is located. Indeed, for a museum to be accredited by a professional body or government, it must prove its documentation system is up to standard. Information about the object is added to a catalogue entry alongside the more practical information necessary for working with the collection within the museum itself.

It is always worth recalling that institutions such as museums, galleries and heritage sites rarely hold comprehensive sets of a particular kind of object, although there are specialist collections with very large collections of specific types of object.[1] The composition of collections is shaped by a variety of factors including the purpose for its foundation and the original contents; decisions made by collectors, donors and curators; the institution's changing priorities and locality; and its resources and size. With this in mind, you should make sure you are aware of the institution's history to better understand the context in which this institution acquired these objects and why certain examples survived. Even the location of the museum, within an urban centre or rural setting, has an influence upon its collection because it determines who its donors and audience are likely to be both today and in the past. A useful document to consult is the institution's acquisition policy, which should outline the collecting remit for objects in an institution's collection and how works will be acquired. In the case of national institutions, these policies should be available online.

Museums

Online catalogues are currently the way in which many researchers initially encounter systems of museum documentation. However, the number of museums with online catalogues is still limited, and even when they do have a 'Collections online' database or similar, this may only represent a portion of the collection. If you are working with an online or printed catalogue, it is necessary to understand the form and function of catalogues and their relation to other forms of documentation in order to make best use of them, and to increase the likelihood of locating appropriate sources. Being conversant with these systems also aids relationships with museum staff as you can use the correct terminology when contacting them.

Accession numbers

An object is given an accession number (also called an inventory number or registration number) when it is accepted into the museum collection, and this will probably be marked somewhere upon the object to identify it. Small objects including coins are not usually marked with the number, but are kept with slips in bespoke trays. These slips must be kept with the object at all times as identification. Accession numbers may simply be a prefix with a letter or letters followed by a number, which is added to sequentially. Some smaller museums use this system but even the Royal Collection has hundreds of thousands of objects in the form of prefix, letters and an ascending number: RCIN441382. Other museums use different prefixes within their collection. These might denote particular bequests or, as in the case of the National Maritime Museum, indicate object type – such as PAD for prints and drawings or FHD for figureheads.

The three-part numbering system which is commonly used incorporates the year of acquisition and gives other information as well. For example, a Swahili woman's arm ornament from Siyu on the East African coast in the British Museum has a number of Af1908,0723.1 The donation was accessioned into the museum in 1908 on 23 July (i.e. 0723), and was the first object registered in that collection. The Af prefix denotes it belongs to the Africa collections, although this categorisation has not been applied consistently throughout the museum during its history. In other three-part cataloguing systems, the second portion of the accession number (0723 in this case) is not a form of the date, but the number of the gift given during that year, rising sequentially with 1 as the first gift/acquisition of the year. If an object is in several parts (e.g. a basket with a lid, a knife with a sheath, or an object broken into pieces), there is usually a suffix in the form of an additional number or a letter. This is important as although these are individual objects, the accession number indicates that they relate to another object. For example, the Yoruba doors discussed in Chapter 2 are numbered as follows: Af1979,01.4546.a (on the right as you look at Figure 2.4) and Af1979,01.4546.b (on the left), while the lintel is Af1979,01.4546.c.

Geographical designations such as the Af prefix do not tell the whole story. For example Af1904,-.290 (Figures 4.1a and 4.1b) was given by the same donor as the arm ornament and also acquired on the East African coast. However, it is a spoon manufactured in China and only arrived in East Africa via trade routes. In this case, the donor included it as part of a large collection of objects from East Africa so it entered the Africa collections, although later donations of Chinese porcelain found in this region were donated to the Asia collections. It is worth being aware that categorisations will vary between institutions and even within the same museum. This example also highlights the varying forms of accession numbers. The date of accession is clear from the number but the rest of the number takes a different form. Figure 4.1b shows how the object was marked with the number at the time of accession (Af1904-290), and the form Af1904,-.290 is used in the online catalogue to ensure that it conforms with the museum's conventional three-part numbering system. While these differences might seem minor, it is very easy to miss objects in catalogues due to these changing conventions in museum recording systems. The basic number will stay the same, but the demands of the digital software may affect the precise format. Digitisation and the development of digital catalogues that sit alongside original, paper-based catalogues mean there is also room for discrepancy between the different catalogue formats.

Numbers which incorporate the year of acquisition are useful especially for researchers interested in collecting history. When scanning museum displays and catalogues you can ascertain quickly when an object arrived at the institution. However, the year indicated in an accession number can also be misleading: the accession date may well not be the date of collection on the spot, particularly if an individual donated collections to the museum late in life or posthumously. Or in other cases, museums might accession unregistered material decades after it arrived in the museum. This is clear with the example of the Yoruba

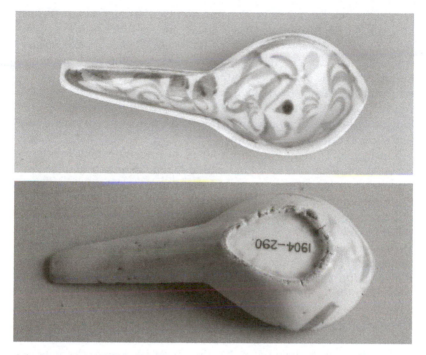

4.1 (a and b) Chinese spoon (top and underside) found on the East African coast, showing the accession number marked on the underside, H: 4 cm, W: 10.2 cm; D: 4.5 cm. Af1904,-.290. © The Trustees of the British Museum.

doors: the British Museum acquired them after the British Empire exhibition in Wembley in 1925 but in the 1970s they were found not to have been assigned a number, so were added to the register at that point. In this case, the information about the delay in accessioning is clearly noted on the catalogue entry, but in other cases the facts might be more obscure.

Not all registration systems function in this way, so check first how the particular institution's system works as this saves much time. In the British Museum, various systems existed concurrently as we have seen above, while departments or specific donors had different arrangements over the course of their history. For example Augustus Wollaston Franks, the influential late nineteenth-century curator of the Department of

Antiquities and Ethnography, donated over 20,000 objects to the British Museum during his tenure. These objects have a wide variety of forms of accession number – such as As,+.8474, OA.2989 or Franks.597.a – depending on the department which received the material and the different numbering conventions at the time. Such systems, and the ways in which they changed, are of great interest to historians of collecting and can be useful for other scholars as they help to illuminate an object's biography by offering clues as to how collections were arranged and perceived at various points in time.

Ideally, object identification numbers do not change, although, on occasion, museums decide to rationalise systems of registration according to trends in practice, curatorial decisions or the restructuring of the museum. This is not encouraged by the International Council of Museums (ICOM) and other museum professional societies. But you will find when dealing with material acquired by museums before the 1960s that objects occasionally have more than one number assigned to them. All previous numbers should be noted in the catalogue so that the present number can be related to the accession register (recording when the object entered the collection with its original number).

The accession register

The accession register sequentially records objects as they enter the collection. It officially documents that the object belongs to the museum and it is a legal document that the museum will rely upon to assert ownership. Accession registers should not be updated or altered. Usually only a small number of people have access to the original copies of accession registers. They are not used for locating material or for general research purposes; the catalogue serves this purpose. However, many museums make several copies of the acquisition register for more regular consultation by staff and researchers. In addition to the accession number, the accession register will include a description of the object (with dimensions), its physical condition and perhaps a drawing or photograph. It will also include the source of the object (culture, region, ethnic group), the date of accession, and acquisition information including the name of the person through which the object was acquired and the mode of acquisition (excavation, collection, gift, purchase, bequest). Museums have a legal responsibility to thoroughly check the provenance of all acquisitions and loans, especially in relation to 'spoliation', when evidence about an object's provenance has been deliberately destroyed, for example material from collections seized under Nazi Germany in 1933–45.

Catalogues

The purpose of the catalogue is two-fold: to store and keep secure information about each object in the collection and to make this information accessible and searchable. Descriptions of objects are essential for identification. There might be many objects which are very similar in form, and to avoid over-reliance on accession numbers marked on the object (which can become illegible through damage) the museum must have another means of identifying the material in its care. The level of detail in the original description may vary according to the convention of the museum and the style of the cataloguer. Many museums have used the transfer to electronic databases as an opportunity to enhance these object descriptions, thus making their collections more searchable and, therefore, useable. The addition of photographs can make detailed descriptions less necessary, but their use may be restricted by copyright.

Catalogues were traditionally written upon cards, and catalogues of this kind still exist in many collections to this day. When retained in card format, they should be arranged in ascending order according to object accession number. Historical cards are retained by all museums even if information has been transcribed onto an electronic database and new acquisitions are recorded electronically. The basic information included on a catalogue record is arranged into different 'fields' for each individual piece of information, including an object's accession number, its name, name of donor and so on. It will also include a full description, its provenance (and people associated with it) and its current condition, as well as a record of any treatment undertaken in the museum and its present location. Other information can include its production information (for example materials and method of manufacture), field collection information, exhibition history and bibliographical information highlighting existing research on this object and its context. Historically, card catalogues also have indexes which enable cross-referencing and they group object numbers by region or object type to aid research across the collection. These indexes, however, do not include all the detailed information present on the object's card in the catalogue.

Electronic catalogues are now standard in many museums where they employ database software to create electronic object records. This has transformed the ability to search for objects and make connections across the collections. This transferral of data is ongoing and responsive to changes in technology. Some museums have changed cataloguing software, which can lead to bulk transfers of data – sometimes by non-experts. Such transcriptions can lead to (occasionally entertaining) errors: in the British Museum, the word 'spear' was misread and entered into the new database as a spoon (of two feet long). Even if electronic databases are available and represent the most efficient way to gather and sift details about a museum's holdings, the original card can be invaluable; changes and updates, which might not appear digitally, shed light on moments in an object's history, as information is added or crossed out.

Using online catalogues

Digital catalogues allow you to search collections to locate appropriate objects. They have transformed the way that researchers think about museum collections and the possibilities for making new connections. Some larger museums now have their catalogue published online. Of these, the British Museum has one of the largest; of the roughly seven million objects in the collection, around 3,500,000 objects are now online and over 900,000 records have one or more images.[2] It is important to remember, however, that this is not the catalogue itself, but a published and searchable selection of it. A limited number of fields are viewable online; information such as storage location is not made public for security reasons. Gallery locations are usually included to encourage visitors to find objects on display.

Online catalogues are an excellent starting point for research as they offer opportunities to swiftly gain a sense of the quantity of a particular object type, period, collector, maker or geographical area within a given collection. Multiple searches must be undertaken with a variety of search terms and spellings to ensure that you find all the possible examples that could be of use to you. When searching catalogues, you are dependent upon the quality and depth of the information on each record. It is worth spending some time establishing the best methods with particular databases if you are to be thorough and methodical; it is easy to miss objects and make assumptions about the quantity or type of object by relying solely on online museum database searches. It is essential to remember that these online catalogues do not represent the entire museum collection. If you visit the museum they may offer you access to the internal catalogue, which will yield more information than you had online. Cross-referencing between the online and card catalogues is extremely useful in these cases; but it is worth recalling that online databases are in effect structured around card catalogues, and an object record represents a card.

The amount of information about an object type may vary from record to record, depending on the demands on the cataloguer at the time of entry. Some databases also include important caches of specific and contextual information about the objects themselves. Depending on the institution, there may be images of the objects or in some cases several views of a single object with x-rays and other associated imagery. Full records of this kind are extremely useful, especially if you have not been able to visit a repository yourself. It is worth noting that such detailed records may be the result of specific research on the object; it is possible this is the result of scientific research, so if you would like to use the information it will be important to check where any results have been published. Your project might use the object differently from the existing published research, but it is worth checking the bibliography fully to ensure that your project is carving a new path.

Be aware that descriptions of similar objects between institutions can vary, such as the way in which natural history drawings are described in the Natural History Museum and the British Library due to their cataloguing parameters and the different needs of the institutions. Similarly, art gallery catalogues present a distinct range of information in line with the requirements of art history. Institutions with mixed collections, such as the National Maritime Museum, have a variety of fields on their online catalogues to ensure they can include the different conventions demanded by each discipline, in this case history of art and history of science. Make sure you remain organised and retain the data that *you* need by keeping a detailed record of your primary sources – in essence, your own database. In this way, you will be able to select relevant and consistent information from these different repositories.

Detailed records on databases are far from the norm. In many cases object records might not have photographs and contain little information beyond basic details. As discussed above, to find out more it will sometimes be necessary to visit the museum to study the written card catalogue and accession registers; information stored on these might not have been transferred to online catalogues. Another strategy for dealing with a scarcity of catalogue information can be to pursue comparative material in other museum collections, and there are also cross-collection databases which use the latest semantic technology to allow you to connect various collections together.[3] Many collections in the USA have excellent online catalogues which could be used to enhance your understanding of artefacts that you have consulted in person, but where you rely on online catalogues rather than first-hand examination, it should be acknowledged within your own study.

Art galleries

Most museums in the UK contain paintings even if their primary collections are three-dimensional objects. However, galleries specialise in paintings, prints, drawings and other two-dimensional artworks, although they may also include objects such as sculpture and furniture. While the focus of this book is not upon the formal analysis of paintings, it is possible that you will need to use galleries or print rooms in your research. Objects in art collections may be the focus of your study or you might use them to help analyse and contextualise other objects (with careful understanding of the art historical context as discussed in Chapters 2 and 5). Key figures in your study might be depicted in portraits, as with the portrait of Joseph Banks surrounded by objects from his collection (see Chapter 2, p. 50). In other cases, figures closely associated with art galleries were also patrons or collectors and participated in scholarly networks, for example George Scharf, Director of the National Portrait Gallery in the nineteenth century, an artist himself. Scharf was also a trustee of the British Museum and his notebooks in the National Portrait Gallery archive include information relating to his time at the British Museum, including drawings of objects and sketches of colleagues made during meetings. As with museums, it is worth being familiar with the history of the institution, how and why it was formed and whether there was a founding collection and set of rinciples and an accessible acquisition policy. This information will help you navigate the relevant records, but it is also important to be acquainted with the specific conventions common to gallery, as opposed to museum, collections.

In terms of organisation of material, it is worth remembering that galleries displaying art within the Western tradition will generally arrange material in their catalogues according to artist; if this is not known then period/school will be attributed. One exception to this could be portrait galleries, where precedence would be given to sitter over artist in the description of works. Item descriptions in the catalogue will include details of the works' dimensions, date and source of acquisition, and current location if on display. In the case of both online and hard-copy catalogues, entries with detailed descriptions will cite bibliographic references for the work. Further information in the catalogue will describe the painting, technique and also the genre and style. These elements are worth remembering if, for example, you are interested in a particular subject, such as how porcelain was displayed in the Low Countries during the early modern period. Historians may, for example, consider the subject matter of the painting, rather than its style, as the most useful aspect for their research. Larger galleries with online collection catalogues may also associate specific-subject terms with particular works, such as elements of costume, furniture, symbolism or even flora and fauna.[4]

Searching a gallery's online database by subject is easy, but when you are using the collection of a smaller gallery without an online searching facility it is worth thinking well in advance about other ways in which to locate the subjects of your enquiry where printed catalogues only allow searches by artist/genre. Galleries tend not to use the three-part system but use single accession or inventory numbers, which are added to sequentially (e.g. N01506 for Millais, *Ophelia* at the Tate Britain). A gallery may also use different series with different prefixed letters to denote sub-collections. As with museums, most galleries will publish some form of annual report including a list of acquisitions for the last year. In addition, printed catalogues may be available. In the case of larger institutions the entire collection of works may be described in a concise catalogue and perhaps in more specific publications that deal in greater detail with works of a certain artistic school, date range or medium within the collection. Galleries will also maintain information on works in their collections (object information files) which form a part of their archives. These files routinely include material relating to the acquisition of works and may also include details of past display, conservation interventions and associated records, such as technical images. As with museums, galleries are likely to display only a percentage of their total collection. When not on display, artworks and paintings will, like objects in museums, have specific storage arrangements, possibly off-site; therefore, if you wish to see paintings that are not on display, leave plenty of time to make an arrangement.

Collections archives

The archives associated with museums and galleries are often complex and fragmented repositories. The catalogues and registers mentioned above might only be the starting point. There may be correspondence, annual reports, conservation reports, drawings, exhibition designs and photographs. Depending on the nature of your study, any of these additional sources might assist you in unravelling the changing ways in which an object has been interpreted, stored and used, and therefore develop your conclusions about its changing meanings.

Correspondence associated with objects may be located in separate places depending upon the institution. In a small museum, it is possible that records of issues pertaining to objects are in the correspondence files of the lead curator or director. In larger institutions, however, this correspondence could be in the archival files of individual departments. Bear in mind that these institutions are reorganised over their years of existence so you will need a good understanding of the history of the institution to know which department acquired the object or collection, and which department that is now. Such files of correspondence may not have been systematically maintained, so you have to be prepared for the possibility that what you are looking for cannot be found. In your attempts to reconstruct correspondence with donors, lenders, auctioneers and other parts of the museum network, it is worth remembering that you may only have one half of the correspondence – in other words, those sent to the museum rather than the outgoing letters.

Annual reports represent the official published record and also provide evidence of the way in which museums communicate with one another, as these are exchanged worldwide. Minutes of meetings can be vital if they reveal discussions about decision-making: for example, whether to acquire objects, the debates around what a particular artefact might mean to the institution and how an artefact might be displayed. This kind of material can help place objects in their institutional context by revealing decision-making and rationale behind the acquisition or rejection of particular objects over time. Explaining the reasons why some kinds of material culture have survived over others is important to historical study and of particular value to studies of the history of collecting.

Visiting collecting institutions

Before finalising an appointment to see objects in a museum, it is generally advised to make a scoping visit. The amount of online information about the contents of the collection and catalogues can vary widely. Some websites may only summarise the contents of the museum, or mention the name of a few key artists or donors. The limitations of researching remotely are clear, and consultation of the main catalogue and communication with museum staff can substantially enhance the quality of research.

Researchers rely heavily upon the expertise of museum staff, whether the curators, researchers or collections/store managers. As mentioned in the Introduction, all publicly owned museums in the UK are regularly reviewed and are subject to cuts in funding. At the time of writing, the museums that have been most seriously hit are those managed by local governments. These cuts in resources can mean that providing access to members of the public to view objects in storage is lower on the list of priorities than keeping the galleries open and fully staffed. To accommodate these difficulties, it is advisable to be patient with your enquiries and plan well in advance. Your initial enquiry may only be met with an automated email promising a reply within a number of weeks. Bear this in mind when creating your research schedule to avoid delays of this kind frustrating your plans.

Another aspect worth considering is how your research might be helpful to the museum. When you use a collection for research, some organisations will expect you to sign an agreement promising to provide copies of any publications that result from the research. Even if this is not the case, it is good practice to offer to share your findings with the museum – especially where material might be relevant for them in terms of provenance of objects, biographical information about collectors, or other issues that relate to the museum. Not all curators have 'research' specified within their job descriptions and therefore appreciate synthesised and up-to-date information about their collections (as long as it has the source of the information clearly indicated). Sharing your findings not only demonstrates your sensitivity to the needs of the museum, but also represents a genuine manifestation of the impact of your research within the public realm. Ensure that you deliver upon promises you make to museums and follow museum guidelines, if provided, on how to present this information. Failing to do so may limit the future opportunities for you and others in researching the collections.

If you find a rich cache of information concerning relevant material either through an online catalogue or from references in other literature, you should make direct contact with the institution. Check the preferred procedure for requesting access to the collections either by consulting the website or making a telephone call. An initial approach to the museum via email asking for further details is standard and this should lead to a visit either to look at their catalogue or to visit the objects, if you already know which these will be. At this point you should think carefully about your research schedule. As mentioned in Chapter 2, the ideal process would be to make a scoping visit to your chosen repositories after an initial appraisal of the secondary literature. In this

Planning

When planning your approach to the museum, consider:

- Is the material on public display? If so, do you need to gain access to the display case or can you see as much as is necessary from the case? Is closer inspection necessary?
- Are you 'ready' to analyse it? Look at Chapter 5 for a summary of the techniques of analysing objects. You may only have one opportunity to handle objects so ensure you are prepared and know what you are looking for and how you will analyse the material.
- How many objects might you want to see? This depends greatly upon the institution, who can guide you, but be realistic (e.g. you may be able to see no more than ten).

way you can assess the quantity of material located in each place, establish how much is on display already and record details of which material you wish to see from the stores, and then make contact with museum staff.

The majority of heritage institutions have a general email address to contact for gaining access. Almost all sizes of museums are heavily over-subscribed in terms of requests for research visits. Large museums have masses of requests nationally and internationally with heavy exhibition and loan programmes to fulfil, while smaller museums manage their diverse workload with limited numbers of staff. This is not to say that you will not be welcomed or your interest and research will not be valued, more that it is essential to allow at least two months from your initial approach to conducting a research visit. Depending on your study, the objects of interest may not all be stored in the same area of the museum – for example, if you are looking at the objects associated with a particular collector, they may be in different departments across the museum, which might require several appointments. Think also about the sizes of objects you hope to see – check the records if possible – as images online can be deceptive, and requesting several large objects which require more than one person to move can place limits on the amount of material you can see.

Depending on the size of the institution, you may meet a curator or a store manager. In both cases, they will be responsible for a wide variety of material so depending on their area of expertise they may or may not be able to answer all of your questions. It is for this reason that you should ensure you inspect the material after completing sufficient secondary reading, to make the most of this moment with the objects themselves.

Heritage sites

Heritage sites include charitable organisations – such as the National Trust, Historic Scotland, Historic England and Historic Royal Palaces – and also private houses open to the public – such as Chatsworth House in Derbyshire. These sites are often filled with objects which have been arranged by curators to give visitors a sense of how a room would have been furnished in a particular period. They are, therefore, fantastic places in which to consider objects spatially: Where were they located? How have they been arranged in response to other objects? Were they displayed against a wall (therefore explaining the design or lack of adornment on one side of the object)? If objects were designed to be used, which other items are located near them, for example desks and writing implements? In this way, the heritage setting can provide helpful contextual information about an object's value and use.

As with museum collections, however, it is always worth thinking critically about the curator's intervention in these displays, which – in turn – depends upon the site itself and its history. Some properties were retained with collections intact (this might well be the case with private houses, which were later donated to charitable organisations) and curators are able to recreate likely arrangements of objects and paintings, according to archival documents associated with the house, including inventories, wills and more recently photographs. Other houses did not come with contents, or only a few select pieces (families may have given them to children or sold them at auction, especially if financial constraints led to the property being given up as a private residence). Organisations such as the National Trust have central repositories of objects and are able to fill gaps across their sites using this resource.

There are several interesting aspects to the relationship between objects and architecture at heritage sites, which affect how we discover and research this material. When presenting a historic house to the public, decisions must be made about which period or periods of history to evoke in the display. The owners may not have retained all the original furniture from earlier periods in the house's history. Curators today may need to draw upon other collections or acquire new items to fill these gaps. In the case of wallpaper, only fragments from a particular period might survive as layers of new fashionable wallpaper are added throughout the house's history. In these cases, contemporary specialists might manufacture new versions of old styles. For historic house curators, this approach gives visitors a greater opportunity to experience the room as it was intended at a particular time, even though the wallpaper is not original. It is more 'authentic' in terms of the experience it offers, although the different kinds of authenticity that can be offered constitute an interesting question to debate.

Historic properties that are under the auspices of larger organisations will most probably have a catalogue. This will collate information about individual objects, and researchers will have consulted historical inventories of the house if these exist. It is likely that curators and volunteers will have researched objects on display, as this work is essential for visitor interpretation. Rarely do individual properties have an online catalogue (the National Trust has an organisation-wide online portal) apart from selected key objects. To ascertain what is in a house before you visit, you should consult any secondary literature which mentions objects connected with the house or its owner, or contact the house manager in advance.

Your approach to researching material culture at heritage sites will depend upon your research questions. A particular object in a property may have been brought to your attention through research elsewhere. As objects are often on permanent display (famous pieces are essential to attracting visitors to the property), you may well be able to see these without an appointment, but it is still worth checking in advance. Such contact may also reveal if a particular guide or volunteer with expertise in this area could be present when you visit. As these properties often have small numbers of staff, they may take time to respond to you, or to locate the individual with the expertise you require. It is worth making an approach early on in your project and factoring in these possible delays in your research plan.

If you are researching the material possessions of a particular figure in the house's history, then you will want to determine the provenance of items in the house. Even if a house is advertised as 'home of X', objects that have no relationship with this person and may have been included in the display to create the appropriate atmosphere, for the reasons outlined above. Determining the relevance of material at the property to your research project will involve consultation with the collections team, house manager or curator in the first instance, who will be likely to have details about the catalogue of objects in that house. If you wish to examine items more closely or handle objects, this might also be the person to consult. For further research, you may be referred to the regional or national specialists. As with museums, follow the guidelines provided on the website or as you are advised by telephone or email.

Private collections

Researchers working on privately held material might be studying it precisely because it has been brought to their attention by the owner – whether through family or a contact. It may also have been possible to see the objects when they were on loan to an exhibition or referred to in a catalogue or book. Even if you have a pre-existing personal contact, which certainly facilitates access, any research upon people's possessions brings its own sensitivities. In making arrangements with owners of historic houses, a fact-sheet or agreement (as advocated by the Oral History Society when conducting interviews[5]) is useful to ensure that you and the owners understand how you will be using the material, where it will be published and that you have permission to use photographs (see also pp. 142–3). Some major private collectors are accustomed to researchers working on their material, have standard procedures and provide access to a catalogue, making the process more straightforward. But in any case, it is important to consider these issues as ethical questions, especially if your research may refer to individuals, ancestors or family members.

If material is held in private collections, this has implications for its accessibility but it also raises important intellectual questions about the composition of that collection. Naturally the negotiation of these issues affects the nature and scope of the enquiry; the selectivity and history of the collection, how it came to the current owners, its condition and so on have to be taken into account when analysing the collection as a whole as well as an individual object. If the owner identifies themselves as a 'collector', they may well be enthusiastic for research to be undertaken on objects in their possession, but it is worth discussing what the particular criteria are for their acquisitions. It is also good practice to record as much of this information as possible in the first instance and then let your research questions and methodology determine how you use this information thereafter. For example, you will want to test the technical accuracy of details provided by owners of collections and your other research might contribute to refining the history of the material. Nonetheless, the ways in which stories or knowledge around an object are shaped and shift over time are rich lines of enquiry and could provide possibilities for future research.

In the case of material that is not held by major private collectors, details of the provenance of an object might only be accessible orally. Therefore, during your visit to a heritage site, ensure that you leave enough time to discuss the material with the owner to establish what the family knows about the objects and how and why they came to own them. You may want to record these discussions using a dictaphone or audio recorder, in which case you must gain permission and commit to using the recording for research purposes only (or if you wish to use it in an exhibition, follow the Oral History Society guidelines). The owners may have conducted research themselves or recorded family connections and stories associated with the material. In all cases you must acknowledge the sources of this information, but also be aware that these accounts may be partial. Your research may challenge some of these established stories about specific artefacts, and when discussing it with owners it is wise to be sensitive to their narrative. You should offer to share material you uncover and the results of any publications.

Exploring other institutions
Depending on the nature of your study, your sources may be located in other places and it is worth considering widely where material may have ended up. Sometimes this will be obvious: for example, studying consumer patterns of the nineteenth century it would be natural to consider department stores, or hospitals for health-related projects. But for many different topics, thinking laterally about what these alternative repositories might offer can produce some rewarding results. For example, if you were looking at the impact of cultural, political or economic phenomena, information on domestic items and their sale can be a useful avenue to explore. Consider, say, whether wallpaper design might show the impact of imperial images and allow you to test the impact of empire at home. Other institutions, such as schools, might relate specifically to studies of the history of education, but it is worth thinking more broadly even if your study is not related to one of these specific areas, as such public institutions themselves offer perspectives on popular experience which can complement the material held in museums and galleries.

Procedures vary for contacting these different institutions, and in approaching them it is useful to remember that, like museums, you will encounter a range of responses to your request to access archives and objects. The department store John Lewis, for example, has its own archive set up for researchers and they are clear about what material is accessible and how it must be used. Organisations may not have

retained comprehensive samples of objects but their archive and catalogues could still provide useful sources for studying the context of
particular categories of material culture. Other commercial outlets may
have changed hands several times; working out the potential location of
extant material can itself be very challenging, even before you establish
if any material of use still exists.

Hospitals are another example of an institution which may possess
interesting historical material culture but they are not places regularly
used by researchers. Their collections might include old scientific instruments and teaching models. It is likely you will encounter various ethical
issues regarding the material you are allowed to see related to named
individuals. The condition of objects and their cataloguing might not
be up to the same standards as those you might find in a heritage institution, and the lack of provenance might limit the amount you can gain
from studying them. However, this material is relatively under-used by
historians and therefore offers possibilities for original and innovative
research.

Associated archival material

Outside the museum, a wealth of other written sources exists which will
enhance your work. Throughout this guide, we have seen how historians
using material culture rely upon written and visual sources in addition
to objects. There are many guides to doing effective archival research,
which are included at the end of this chapter and also in the Select
Bibliography. For example, if you have been studying objects owned by
a particular person, then their official and personal papers (including
correspondence, diaries or visual sources) will be essential for tracing
an object's history.

There are particular 'object-specific' written sources which can be
extremely useful, an excellent example of which are legal documents
such as probate inventories. These were drawn up at the time of a
person's death, listing the belongings of a person and their monetary
value.[6] A significant body of literature has exposed the wide range of
findings such documents can reveal, in particular about the changing
patterns of consumption over time.[7] In studies of the early modern
period, thousands of probate inventories have been examined by a variety of scholars to trace 'an ever-multiplying world of goods, a richly
varied and complex material culture'.[8] Much of this literature examines

broader economic patterns of production and consumption derived from these sources. Others, such as Lorna Weatherill, combine a study of the material evidence alongside the inventory to explore the meaning of consumer behaviour – moving the focus from production to the activities and experiences of consumers.[9] Nigel Goose and Nesta Evans alert us to the care we must take when using such sources: their survival is fragmentary, and it was certainly not possible for everyone to draw up a will so wealthy men are disproportionately represented.[10] Nonetheless, these documents have the great potential to open up the material world of a household and can usefully be used in tandem with other archival, visual and material sources.

These kinds of document are more likely to be stored in local or national archives and an increasing number are now available online. For example, Professor John Montias, an art historian, amassed a vast collection of inventories from Amsterdam in the seventeenth century – particularly of artists' homes but also of other figures. This collection is now on an online database which is an incredibly useful resource for material culture historians and those examining the Golden Age in Dutch history.[11] As with all textual primary sources, these must be analysed thoroughly considering the purpose and context of their production as well as the content.

There are increasing numbers of written sources online, including archives and historical books. As with all online sources, you should be careful to note the limitations that this might impose upon your research and be sure of the provenance of the material. Official national and institutional archives with classmarks are reliable repositories, as are central databases, but as with all historical research the use of online sources should be undertaken with care, ensuring as far as possible that the material is genuine and has been scanned or transcribed correctly.[12]

Photographs and printed visual sources
We have discussed in other chapters the importance of understanding objects in different contexts and noted the usefulness of analysing visual material in art galleries. Photographs are another category of visual source which might prove critical in your research. Photographs must also be treated as cultural constructions (rather than as presenting absolute 'truths') and analysed accordingly. Deborah Cohen's study of the domestic interior in Victorian Britain draws upon rich and varied photographic collections.[13] Part of the success of Cohen's analysis lies in her attendance to the reasons why these images were created in the first

place. The wide variety of skills and methods associated with analysing photographs is beyond the scope of this guide but it is worth noting that photograph albums can usefully be analysed as material objects with their own production history and many still bear the traces of their use. Methodologies (as discussed in Chapter 3) and analytical techniques (in Chapter 5) can be employed to analyse albums as objects. We discussed these issues briefly in the Introduction when considering our definitions of material culture; if using albums, you should consider to what extent you will analyse individual photographs, or focus upon the assemblage of images together.

Our concern here, however, is in locating these sources. A theme throughout this book has been the ways in which one can trace the creation, use, display and movement of objects as a way of understanding their meaning and the society within which they were made and used. Naturally, photographs are vital sources for such investigations for studies from the mid-nineteenth century onwards. However, we must remain mindful of the status of photography and the particular techniques and conventions applied when analysing objects in photographs. For example, in portrait photographs, objects might have symbolic meaning or, conversely, might merely be a prop in a photographer's studio. Objects present within photographs of interiors might be carefully curated, or may be moved from their original position to create a pleasing composition or framing device. Therefore, as with text, all such interventions with the image must be taken into account when interrogating the meaning of objects in photographs.

Museums include photographs as part of their collections, such as those by famous photographers or images of significant figures. However, museum archives also often contain a wealth of photographs from a variety of sources – collecting expeditions, exhibition displays and images of individual objects – in the form of lantern slides, negatives as well as printed photographs. Even if these do not include images of actual objects, the contextual information about the people and the way in which objects were acquired can be illuminating. As noted above, accessing museum archives can take time. Remember that photographs may be stored separately from other objects or they may simply not have been retained.

Newspapers, magazines, adverts and other printed materials also include images which can be of great use to historians. In the late nineteenth century, images within the *Illustrated London News* regularly featured objects to interest their readers, for example from recent archaeological excavations in the UK and overseas. They also reported on expeditions across the world. In these cases London-based artists often created the published engravings from photographs sent to the capital, and alterations may have been made. Adverts allude to the values associated with material things and the ways in which they attempted to persuade consumers to purchase goods can be revealing. Many of these publications are now online and therefore a material culture-driven approach can exploit these more easily accessible sources with the requisite methodological care.

ETHICAL QUESTIONS

Museums and other stores are bound by a series of ethical guidelines to which you must adhere. Their duty is to care for their collections; therefore, there may be practical reasons or conservation requirements which mean you cannot access objects. There may also be ethical issues associated with handling or using the objects. Those associated with human remains may also have restrictions about what you can research or reproduce in print. As noted above, in other institutions such as hospitals and schools, you should be careful to check the ethical codes of these organisations which may involve named individuals. When consulting private collections, ensure you acquire the written consent of your participants to research and publish this material. When discussing the cultures of indigenous peoples around the world, look through the most recent literature on your area and use the names and terms which those groups and ethnic communities choose for their own identification. The original labels and records in museums are likely to be outdated and may have colonial associations.

IN SUMMARY

This chapter has given detailed guidance on navigating collections, locating objects within them and arranging to visit the material in question. It has also sought to de-mystify the processes by which collections are compiled and arranged in order to provide useful insights into the context in which a researcher must work. If you approach your research planning with these issues in mind, you will improve your chances of accessing objects of interest alongside items that you had not ever imagined you would find. The next chapter discusses the techniques that can be used to analyse material culture.

NOTES

1 See, for example, The Fan Museum in London: www.thefanmuseum. org.uk [accessed 20 January 2016].
2 Data drawn from: www.britishmuseum.org/research/collection_ online/search.aspx [accessed 16 October 2015].
3 See for example the Europa project: www.europeana.eu/portal/ [accessed 21 January 2016].
4 Depth of cataloguing will vary, but for an extremely detailed example see Tate's description of N01506 Sir John Everett Millais, Bt, Ophelia: www.tate.org.uk/art/artworks/millais-ophelia-n01506 [accessed 20 January 2016].
5 These guidelines can be found at www.ohs.org.uk/advice/ethical-and-legal [accessed 21 September 2016].
6 T. Arkell, N. Evans and N. Goose (eds), *When Death Do Us Part: Understanding and interpreting the probate records of early modern England* (Oxford: Leopard's Head Press, 2000).
7 J. Brewer and R. Porter (eds), *Consumption and the World of Goods* (London: Routledge, 1993); J. Whittle, M. Overton, D. Dean and A. Hann, *Production and Consumption in English Households, 1600–1750* (London: Routledge, 2004).
8 Jan de Vries, 'Purchasing Power and the World of Goods: Understanding the household economy in early modern Europe', in Brewer and Porter (eds), *Consumption and the World of Goods,* pp. 85–132, p. 89.
9 Weatherill, *Consumer Behaviour and Material Culture.*
10 N. Goose and N. Evans, 'Wills as a Historical Source', in Arkell, Evans and Goose (eds), *When Death Do Us Part,* pp. 38–71.
11 The database can be found at the Frick Collection: http://research. frick.org/montias/home.php [accessed 21 January 2016].
12 For a discussion of the issues with digitisation, see A. Prescott, 'The Imaging of Historical Documents', in M. Greengrass and L. Hughes (eds), *The Virtual Representation of the Past* (Aldershot: Ashgate, 2008), pp. 7–22.
13 D. Cohen, *Household Gods: The British and their possessions* (London: Yale University Press, 2006).

RECOMMENDED FURTHER READING

Akin, Marjorie, 'Passionate Possession: The formation of private collections', in W.D. Kingery (ed.), *Learning from Things: Method and theory of material culture studies* (Washington, DC: Smithsonian Institution Press, 1996), pp. 102–28.

Bounia, Anna, 'Codes of Ethics and Museum Research'. *Journal of Conservation and Museum Studies* 12:1 (2014): www.jcms-journal.com/articles/10.5334/jcms.1021214 [accessed 28 January 2016].

Collections Trust guide to catalogues: www.collectionstrust.org.uk/media/documents/c1/a216/f6/CataloguingFactsheet.pdf [accessed 28 January 2016].

Foster, Janet, and Julia Sheppard (eds), *British Archives: A guide to archive resources in the United Kingdom* (London: Palgrave, 2002).

Gunn, Simon, and Lucy Faire (eds), *Research Methods for History* (Edinburgh: Edinburgh University Press, 2011).

Historic England archives (which include resources on historic buildings and social history, including photographs, drawings, reports and publications from the 1850s to the present day, across the UK): www.historicengland.org.uk/images-books/archive [accessed 28 January 2016].

ICOM guidance on registering objects (CIDOC Fact Sheet 1): www.network.icom.museum/fileadmin/user_upload/minisites/cidoc/DocStandards/CIDOC_Fact_Sheet_No_1.pdf [accessed 28 January 2016].

ICOM guidance on numbering and marking objects (CIDOC Fact Sheet 2): http://icom.museum/fileadmin/user_upload/pdf/Guidelines/CIDOC_Fact_Sheet_No2.pdf [accessed 28 January 2016].

Manias, Chris, 'Feature Archive: A guide to museum archives': www.frenchhistorysociety.co.uk/blog/?p=437 [accessed 1 July 2015].

Thompson, John M., and Douglas A. Bassett, *A Manual of Curatorship: A guide to museum practice*, 2nd edition (Oxford and Boston, MA: Butterworth-Heinemann, 1992).

✦ 5 ✦

ANALYSING SOURCES

There are many different ways of accessing information about material culture through observation, examination and other forms of investigation. This chapter will work through the main methods of analysis you might wish to use when you work with objects. It is possible, of course, that you will need to use several methods to help you answer your research question. Here, the opportunities and constraints of examining objects in person will also be discussed. The chapter is arranged in sections: the first deals with methods of investigating objects physically, the second section moves on to consider contextual research and the last section discusses ways to further extend the research process on the basis of the first two modes of analysis.

Jules Prown's method
1. Description (based on observation): build a list of materials, dimensions and iconographic/decorative features.
2. Deduction (based on sensory engagement): consider what the object does and how it does it.
3. Speculation: think creatively to form hypotheses.
4. Emotional response: link the object to experiences and feelings.
5. Programme of research: what would you need to do next to prove or disprove your hypothesis about an object?

When first approaching material culture research, there are some basic exercises that can be employed to help develop analytical skills in relation to the material properties of the sources encountered. For example, back in the early 1980s the art historian Jules Prown elucidated an approach to studying objects that worked through a close analysis of the object itself in order to get to a better understanding of the object's social and cultural context.[1] Acknowledging that many researchers felt de-skilled in the detailed examination of objects as opposed to texts, Prown suggested a protocol that moved from description, through deduction and, finally, on to speculation – forcing the researcher through a process of close looking and describing before allowing consideration of the object's context to come to the fore. Whilst Prown's approach has been widely used for several decades, this concern with accessing the material qualities of an object before negotiating its cultural or social meanings is no less important today than it was in the 1980s. Examples of such contemporary approaches to studying the material qualities of objects will be discussed in order to provide the reader with a range of ways of decoding artefacts by first engaging with their material characteristics.

Try this exercise at home

Take any household object and ignore your contextual knowledge of it. You will find yourself thinking more carefully about its form: 'a curved section serves as a handle', 'the handle is made from wood and the body of the object is made from metal'.

Or, imagine describing it to someone who cannot see it and has no prior knowledge of the culture from which it comes.

Other similar protocols have been developed by scholars working in history and art history, many of which focus strongly on the material presentation of the object in question. For example, Gregg Finley has suggested an approach that works from the object's construction (its material composition and the techniques that were used in its construction) through to its social, economic or cultural meanings in the society in which it was produced.[2] This approach places less emphasis on your personal or emotional response as a researcher to the object and stresses, instead, the use of physical evidence to deduce context. Ray Batchelor, on the other hand, breaks things down further by suggesting an approach that deals separately with the reason for the object, its material, the way in which it was made, its significance as a commodity, its design and, lastly, its use.[3] See Figure 5.1 for a comparison of three different protocols to object analysis, as described by Finley, E. McClung Fleming and Batchelor.

PHYSICAL EXAMINATION

Handling an original artefact is one of the best ways to gain a full understanding of its material qualities and the way in which it was constructed and used. However, such a direct interaction is not always possible (sometimes researchers are not able to touch the object in question) and, in most cases, engagement with an object will be mediated in some way. In a museum setting, for example, it is most likely that a researcher will be closely supervised by a member of curatorial staff and objects will be encountered in a space designed to keep them safe – including plastazote coverings on tables, gloves to wear, and a range of rules to abide by for safe object handling. When you begin to study material culture in person, it is helpful to be aware of the conventions around handling objects. Practice, however, is not uniform across collections and the material, age, rarity and institutional context of the object will all affect the way in which a researcher is able to engage with it in person. Indeed, for some kinds of material culture – particularly visual culture such as paintings, prints and drawings – it is not usual to touch the piece at all. In these cases, researchers will be expected to engage in a process of close looking but will not usually be allowed to handle the item.

When you are able to handle an object of interest in a given collection, there are some general guidelines to be aware of:

1. Make sure your hands are clean and dry before handling objects and that all jewellery that could come into contact with the object is removed.
2. You may be asked to wear cotton or nitrile gloves depending on the material you are handling and the preference of the museum or collection. On the whole, manuscripts and rare books can be handled without gloves (because gloves can decrease dexterity and cause damage to the artefact) whereas metal objects will often require gloves (because the oils on our hands can react with the metal and cause damage). Some museums prefer porcelain to be handled without gloves because of the slippery nature of the surface and the better grip of bare hands.
3. Always hold the object over the table or surface which has been provided (preferably plastazote, sometimes acid-free tissue paper).
4. Use both hands to handle the object and do not pick it up by a weak point, such as a handle, or a secondary or protruding part.

Here, we will walk through the range of circumstances that you are likely to encounter when researching material culture up-close, explain the reasons for this variety in practice and offer suggestions for how to get the best out of direct encounters with original artefacts. If your study is

G. Finley, 'The Gothic Revival and the Victorian Church in New Brunswick: Toward a strategy for material culture research', *Material Culture Bulletin* 32 (1990), 1–16.	E. McClung Fleming, 'Artifact Study: A proposed model', *Winterthur Portfolio* 9 (1974), 153–73.	R. Batchelor, 'Not Looking at Kettles', in S. Pearce (ed.), *Interpreting Objects and Collections* (London: Routledge, 1994), pp. 139–43.
1. **Construction**: consider the dimension, proportions, style, decoration condition, fabrication and quality of craftsmanship.	1. **Identification**: establish the distinctive features e.g. classification, authentication and description.	1. **The idea** or the invention: what is this object for?
		2. **The material**: what is it made from?
2. **Function**: think through why the object was created and how it was used.	2. **Evaluation**: use comparison with other similar objects to make further judgements.	3. **Making** or manufacture: what techniques or technologies were used in its production?
3. **Provenance**: develop a chronological story (where and when the object was used; who created, owned or used it).	3. **Cultural analysis**: examine the relationship of the object with its culture of origin.	4. **Marketing**: what is this object's broader commercial context?
4. **Significance**: identify the object's meaning(s) in its earlier contexts. What did it mean to its makers, owners and users?	4. **Interpretation**: what is the object's meaning in relation to our own culture?	5. **Art**: what design or decorative features can you identify and what do they mean?
		6. **Use**: is there any physical evidence of how the object has been used?

Figure 5.1 Object analysis protocols

confined to photographs or digital reproductions, you can try as far as possible to follow these guidelines. Once you are ready to work with the object, there are various ways you can investigate it with your eyes, your hands and also with tools. If you intend to conduct a full examination of an object, it might be helpful to bring with you some or all of the following equipment: tape measure, magnifying glass, camera, weighing scales, pencil and paper.

Observation and description

When starting to work with an object, it is good practice to begin with close observation leading to a detailed description of its physical attributes. Whilst it is tempting to feel that you can take in the key characteristics of an object very quickly, spending time on close observation and description holds real rewards, as small details come to the fore and immediate assumptions can be tested. Look at it from all angles. Look for marks of production, use, display and damage. Observation can be conducted with the eyes alone, but when it comes to recording your observations some equipment can be very useful. For example, a magnifying glass comes in handy if you need to identify an object through a small maker's mark, or if close examination of the surface can illuminate the place of origin or process of manufacture. Some researchers even use small, hand-held microscopes for research visits, providing an even more detailed view of the material composition of the object.

As you are looking at the object, start to make a record of its features. There are many different ways of going about this and you should do this in the way best suited to your research project. However, one example is shown in Figure 5.2a. Another way of recording your object is to work through different fields of information – writing down as much detail as possible in each section – as shown in the example in Figure 5.2b.

Scientific analysis

By and large, historians are unlikely to use invasive or scientific methods of material analysis and careful observation can provide a wealth of information. However, if you do need to know more than the eye can discern about the raw materials used or the sources of those materials, then it might be useful to employ some technology. In most cases,

Name: *ceramic pot*
Short general description: *round, earthenware glazed pot with handles*
Material(s): *earthenware, slip, glaze*
Sketch of diagram (add dimensions and annotations where helpful):

Dimensions: *Height: 146mm, Width (at widest point): 151mm, Diameter of mouth: 115mm, Diameter of base: 72mm*
Place of origin (if known):
Date of manufacture (if known):

Physical description:

Parts and components:

Materials and techniques: *silver*

Marks and inscriptions: *maker's mark on base*

Condition: *repairs to hinge*

Dimensions:

Function:

Location: *current: north gallery, Bradbury Museum; original: London*

Collection information:

Associated objects:

5.2 (a and b) Object records. Sketch of earthenware pot by Joey O'Gorman. Reproduced with permission.

historians will rely upon the existing work of specialist scientists and con-servators for these avenues of research. For example, using a microscope can illuminate features such as minute abrasions, which are revealing of the ways in which the object has been used. Likewise, microscopy pro-vides a nearer view of the object's molecular structures – which can, in turn, provide valuable data on the materials, their origins and processes of manufacture.[4] Other techniques, such as radiography (x-ray), can be used to decipher the chemical composition of a particular object. Sometimes, archaeologists will take small samples of an object in order to test its composition or to detect very small amounts of a particular material.[5] These technologies have been adapted to become more user-friendly and tools such as hand-held X-ray fluorescence spectrometers are now commonly used by archaeologists.[6]

RECORDING

As opportunities to look at or handle objects in person can be limited, quick methods of documenting the physical aspects of an object are really useful to the researcher. Obviously, photography provides the quickest and most accurate visual representation, but, as noted above, drawing objects and making a detailed record of their physical dimensions and qualities brings other advantages. There are various considerations to make when choosing a method of recording a particular object and these will be explored in full in this section. In particular, issues relating to pho-tography will be discussed, from practical tips on achieving a good record of an object with a digital camera through to the constraints placed on the use of particular images in different circumstances, for example pub-lishing. Drawing as a method of recording objects for research purposes will also be considered and a protocol for technical drawing derived from archaeological practice will be offered as one possible option. Of course, it is also possible to use less rigorous forms of sketching to help you remember the key features of an object without fulfilling the more elaborate requirements of technical drawing.

Drawing

There are a number of advantages to drawing rather than photograph-ing an object. For one, it gives you the chance to record and highlight details that might be of particular interest to you, such as the thickness of a ceramic pot's walls, the diameter of its base or an aspect of decoration or damage. For example, in Chapter 3 we discussed a study of working-class needlework in nineteenth-century England for which the researcher, Vivienne Richmond, had executed a detailed sketch of an object she found in the archive (see p. 81). While drawing your object you are able to focus closely and consistently on its features in a way that is unlikely when taking a photograph, and this level of close observation can enhance your overall object analysis. During the process of drawing, it is common to discover features of the object of which you were not aware when you simply observed its form.

First, depending on the size and complexity of the object in hand, you may wish to make a decision about the scale of your drawing in relation to the original – for example, opting for a 1:2 ratio. You will also need to think about how many views of the object you wish to draw, such as the front, back, top, bottom or even a section. A section is an imaginary view of the object, usually cut across its breath or sometimes its length in order to reveal features such as the thickness of the wall or the interior of a vessel.[7]

There are common conventions relating to archaeological artefact drawing, including the use of particular kinds of cross-hatching to denote an imaginary view of a section of an object. Likewise, it is usual to depict objects with a light source in the top left-hand corner and to shade the object accordingly. Changes of tone or texture are sometimes indicated with pencil lines or dots. However, for most historians who are not producing technical drawings for publication, this level of conformity to convention should not be necessary. Nevertheless, using archaeological approaches to drawing artefacts to record their key features can be very useful and can be combined, where helpful, with photographs of the same object, each technique capturing a different range of qualities. For example, you could use a drawing to delineate a pattern visible on the surface of an object, whether engraved, embroidered or painted. Similarly, if the previous use of an object is important to your research, using a drawing to emphasise areas of damage could also be helpful. Annotations might note aspects which are more difficult to describe through drawing, such as textures, colours and dimensions.

Photography

Today, large-scale photography of museum objects often takes place in the context of digitisation, which is helping to make object collections more accessible via searchable online catalogues.[8] However, museums like the V&A have a long history of photographing artefacts and from the earliest days of the Museum there has been a photographic studio for this purpose. Photography remains a very useful tool for the researcher, especially in the context of visits to view collections where time is limited. Ensure in advance of your visit that you are aware of the institutional rules regarding photography or that you have permission from the object's owner. In these circumstances, taking pictures with a basic camera without any special equipment can usefully document a research visit for future reference. If you have time and equipment at your disposal, however, a more professional effect can be achieved and you can record objects from different angles and produce images that are appropriate for subsequent publication. Here we will provide some guidance to taking high-quality images.

Use the best-quality camera that you have access to and, ideally, one which allows adjustment of the shutter speed and the aperture, with a powerful lens and a good zoom. Prepare to take your photographs by first managing the set-up:

1. Locate a surface against a wall that can provide a suitable backdrop to your photograph and a stable space to place objects.
2. Set up your camera on a tripod.
3. Set up directed lighting that can clearly illuminate the objects to be photographed – this could be from natural light or lamps.

	Equipment
stable surface	✓
digital camera	✓
tripod	✓
light(s)	✓
backdrop (e.g. plain white)	✓

If you are planning to take many pictures, it is worth spending some time setting up your photography space to make sure that you can move objects easily and safely from one place to another and establish a methodical and time-efficient approach. You may want to photograph objects in a systematic way, capturing the front view of each. However, it is worth considering that when you photograph complex objects, it can be preferable to situate them at an angle so that you can see their features more distinctly. The decisions you make about the number of photographs you take of each object and the aspects of those objects that you most wish to capture will largely depend on the research questions you are trying to answer. Of course, it is also possible that you will simply use the images as an aid to memory when you are writing up your research findings or as images within the text of your piece to illustrate particular points within your argument.

Digital imaging and three-dimensional scanning

Digital imaging and three-dimensional scanning techniques are becoming increasingly accessible to researchers and can enhance both our documentation and understanding of objects. Different approaches are available, including reflected infrared imaging, photogrammetry and three-dimensional (3-D) scanning, which are rapidly becoming widely accessible technologies that are finding new roles within museums and heritage environments.[9] Infrared imaging has tended to be used primarily for analysis of paper and painted surfaces. However, photogrammetry is an increasingly low-cost, accessible and portable technique that is applied widely in material culture research, especially by archaeologists. The key to photogrammetry is that it turns 2-D images into 3-D models by producing a large amount of 3-D surface data from a small number of photographs taken with what is now fairly standard equipment. On the other hand, 3-D scanning machines use triangulation to determine the shape of a given object in three-dimensional space, and the data they produce can be used to create highly accurate, digital visualisations of a given object. Whilst it is unlikely that a museum or collection will have 3-D models of all of their objects, using either photogrammetry or a 3-D scanner to produce some digital objects is becoming common practice within collections.[10] Such a resource might be useful to you during your research because it can offer remote access to the object 'in the round'. Some museums are also creating 3-D prints of their objects; these can provide new opportunities for handling and alternative ways of investigating the materiality of the object.[11] Of course, there are many differences between studying an original artefact and a 3-D reproduction of that object. A 3-D model cannot tell you what the object is made of or what it looks like to the naked eye. However, 3-D models can be digitally manipulated to help you understand particular features of the object better. For example, a 3-D model might help you understand how different parts of an object fit together or it might be possible to contextualise the object by placing it into a reconstruction of historical space.

As more and more 3-D models are created by collections, new opportunities arise for researchers to use and re-use these complex data sets to help them answer different questions. Technological development is also very rapid at this time and the field of 3-D imaging is likely to change quickly over the coming years and decades. By engaging with our expanding digital media, and the kinds of knowledge they offer, we will ultimately enhance our understanding of the material world. Moreover, it is almost certain that these powerful methods of visualising material culture will also have ramifications for the ways in which researchers present their findings and communicate material culture history to wider audiences.

DRAWING CONCLUSIONS

Depending on your confidence with identifying materials and manufacturing techniques, the conclusions you draw from a physical examination of an object may be more or less provisional. Nevertheless, building as firm a picture as possible on the basis of observation and recording will help you use other sources of information to verify your initial findings. The materials that compose a particular object and the techniques used in its production are key pieces of evidence that can help you to unlock an object's meaning – particularly in relation to its origins and purpose. For example, you might observe that an object is made from metal, but it may prove difficult to determine whether that metal is bronze, brass or copper. Chemically, the differences between them are that copper is a pure metal (an element) found in nature, whereas brass (copper and zinc) and bronze (copper and tin) are alloys produced by humans.[12] Colour or patina can, of course, be helpful indications in this case but if you are still unsure then you might be able to make an educated guess based on the kind of object you are looking at. For example, copper is more typically employed for utilitarian, rather than decorative, purposes, such as plumbing. Brass is often used, at least in part, for its decorative characteristics, for objects such as locks, doorknobs and fire irons. However, brass is also a common material for ammunition casings. Historically, bronze has been used for functional objects such as axe heads and it has also had a range of industrial uses,[13] but in the early modern and modern periods it is generally found in the form of decorative or art objects, particularly sculpture. Of course, there will always be exceptions to the rule, but thinking about the purpose of the given object and, also, its probable age can help you to draw more reliable conclusions about the materials that it is made from and then any meanings associated with these materials.

Similarly, some methods of production are time-period specific and can help you to narrow down not only an object's likely place and date of origin, but also its material composition. For example, during the nineteenth century glass-moulding techniques were adapted repeatedly to make mass production increasingly effective. Previously glass bottles had been blown and shaped by hand. As a result of moving from hand-making to moulding glass bottles, those made in the nineteenth century can be accurately dated by looking at the seam created by the mould. In the middle of the century, moulds were only created for the main body of the bottle, excluding the neck, which was created by hand in the traditional way. As the century progressed, moulds were further adapted to shape part of the neck of the bottle and, subsequently, the whole bottle top to bottom. As you work with material culture, your skills of material analysis will improve as you become familiar not only with the qualities of particular materials but also the ways in which they age over time and the uses they were commonly put to in different periods and places. Moreover, where catalogue entries exist, details of materials and technique are very likely to be recorded and this can help you assess the accuracy of initial conclusions.

Additional evidence of an object's material composition and life history can be deduced from signs of use or adaptation. For example, something as simple as a chip in the rim of an otherwise robustly manufactured drinking vessel might support the supposition that the object had been used, or even heavily used, during its lifetime. The places in which an object has sustained damage are also significant, providing evidence of patterns of use that may be unfamiliar to us in the twenty-first century. Some kinds of deterioration in an object's integrity happen slowly over time and are not specifically caused by use. For example, in general porcelain retains its glaze, and therefore its colour, very well over long periods of time, but if a porcelain bowl were to spend years buried underground its glaze might become so seriously degraded that the object might lose its original colour. Even in better conditions, porcelain is subject to crackle lines across its surface; these are minute cracks in the glaze which can turn yellow or brown with age. Whilst these signs of age may not allow you to make a very precise prediction of the date of manufacturing, it can still help to ascertain that an object is not a recently made artefact.

Some objects may have been mended or even adapted at some point in their history. Damage, repairs and adaptations can reveal a lot about the materials, techniques, uses and changing value of an object over time. For example, a repair to a handle of a jug suggests the object's ongoing utility (practical, aesthetic or emotional) to its owner; it might also reveal this individual's skills in mending household objects. Some adaptations to objects can confuse the modern observer, making the object difficult to attribute to a particular time or place. For example, where a wooden chair has been embellished with additional decorative features or had its surface re-worked, it might prove more difficult to disentangle the original from the adapted features or to place the object within its relevant contexts. Again, this is the kind of dilemma that can often be resolved with reference to the catalogue, as adaptations are likely to be recorded and, sometimes, explained in these records. It is also worth remembering that whilst most objects conform to a 'type' – which in turn corresponds with particular materials, techniques and a specific place and time of origin – some artefacts will confound our standard categories and will present features that are atypical. This pro-vides another reason to keep an open mind when you initially consult an object, however prosaic, because even modest, everyday goods can present idiosyncratic features, especially when they have been hand-made and adapted over time.

When consulting objects that reside in collections, or have done so in the past, it is worth looking for any signs of the object's history as part of one or more collections. Such clues are usually visible on the surface of the object as accession numbers; in addition, it is sometimes possible to discern previous conservation work. Efforts to conserve or even restore artefacts usually leave their mark.[14] Moreover, techniques that were commonly used in the nineteenth or twentieth centuries have often been found to cause damage to the integrity of the original arte-fact. When examining an object, therefore, it is possible to encounter evidence of early twentieth-century efforts to preserve it alongside twenty-first-century attempts to undo the damage caused by earlier interventions and stabilise the object for the future. Detrimental restoration techniques can make objects much more difficult to research. For example, rare books and manuscripts have been collected by private collectors and institutions for centuries and have been subject to generation after generation of efforts to preserve or improve the physical appearance of texts that have suffered over time. Paper is particularly susceptible to environmental changes and can be easily destroyed or damaged by water or fire. To preserve old paper, nineteenth- and early twentieth-century specialists would often use a method called 'silking' to reinforce the fragile pages with a layer of silk gauze, applied with paste. It was thought that this process would enable the paper to better withstand warm or wet climates. However, in many cases the silk itself would deteriorate, shrink or come away from the paper – making the manuscript or book less readable. This example is relatively easy to identify, but many other forms of conservation or restoration are less clearly recognisable and can confuse the observer in their understanding of the object's original state. That said, where treatments can be observed they can provide evidence of the object's history within one or more collections, where such practices were most likely to occur. Again, catalogue entries are very likely to record details relating to previous conservation and this is worth consulting if you are in any doubt.

A more clear-cut sign of an object's history within a collection is an accession number either written directly onto the object itself or attached as a label. As discussed in Chapter 4, objects are usually only given one accession number when they enter a collection and so where an object has more than one, it is very likely that it has resided in more than one collection over time. Sometimes accession numbers incorporate the year in which the object was accessioned and so it is sometimes possible to use this evidence to date an object's collection history very precisely (although recourse to the accession register may be necessary). Moreover, accession numbers can be used to connect objects with other artefacts or groups of objects, which, in turn, can provide valuable evidence of both the object's origins and its different 'life stages', residing in a range of social or institutional contexts.

Situating an object within a collection, past or present, can be useful for more than one reason. Not only can you learn about the object's movements and meanings over different periods of time, but you might also be able to use this information to put it into context. It is possible that the object you are studying is the only one of its kind in that collection, but it is more likely that there will be several examples. Traditionally, collectors have tended to source many examples of the same types of object in order to be able to amass a greater body of evidence about its form or function and to be able to make comparisons between individual examples. This is a real advantage when studying material culture because it means that you can often find many comparable examples of a particular kind of object within one collection, without having to use many different collections in different geographical locations.[15] For example, on encountering a pair of early modern Italian 'chopines' – fashionable shoes with large platform soles – in The Metropolitan Museum of Art's collections, it is difficult to determine what the key features are of this kind of shoe and how to reliably recognise a chopine as compared to, say, a Japanese 'geta' (also featuring a platform sole) or a Turkish 'nalın' bathing clog, with its similar front strap (Figure 5.3). Only by consulting other examples of chopines does it become clear that they vary quite considerably in design and material composition. Of the three late sixteenth- and early seventeenth-century examples in The Metropolitan Museum of Art's collections, the fabric is variously of leather and silk and the shoes are ornamented with a punched pattern in the case of the leather pair, and lace in the case of the silk examples (Figures 5.4 and 5.5).[16]

5.3 Pair of chopines (c. 1550–1650), Italy, silk and metal, 12.7 cm by 22.9 cm. 2009.300.1494a, b. Brooklyn Museum Costume Collection at The Metropolitan Museum of Art, Gift of the Brooklyn Museum, 2009; Gift of Herman Delman, 1955.

5.4 Pair of chopines (c. 1600), Italy, leather, silk and wood; heel to toe: 22.2 cm. 1973.114.4a, b. The Metropolitan Museum of Art, Purchase, Irene Lewisohn Bequest, 1973.

5.5 Pair of chopines (1590–1610), Italy, silk and metal, 12.7 cm by 22.9 cm. 2009.300.1408. Brooklyn Museum Costume Collection at The Metropolitan Museum of Art, Gift of the Brooklyn Museum, 2009; Gift of Mrs Clarence R. Hyde, 1928.

By comparing and contrasting the chopines with objects categorised similarly and differently it becomes possible to gain an understanding of the key identifying characteristics, the level of variation in design and the relationship between this particular kind of shoe and other varieties with comparable features. In so doing, wider questions of regional variation, material composition and decorative scheme can all begin to be addressed.

CONTEXTUAL RESEARCH

Having conducted a thorough physical examination of an object or group of objects, recorded their characteristics in detail and begun to draw conclusions from the evidence in front of you, the next step is to locate any further contextual information you need to corroborate aspects of your analysis. As mentioned above, the catalogue entry is the most likely first port of call, as it commonly provides valuable information on materials, techniques, location of origin, circumstances of acquisition and collection history.[17] You may, in fact, have first encountered the object via its catalogue entry and this information is quite likely to shape your investigation of the object in person. However, in some cases catalogue entries may either be lacking or extremely brief, leaving you to seek out other sources of contextual information. If you are consulting an object in the presence of the curator, you could ask for suggestions either in terms of what is likely to be the case or where it might be possible to look for further information; this could be other objects in the same collection, objects in other collections or reading on this category of artefact. In the absence of any collection-specific documentation or curatorial knowledge, then, it is worth searching online catalogues to discover if another collection might have comparable objects with more detailed accompanying records.

Once you have established as much as you can about the particular object you are studying, it might be helpful to consult some more specialised literature on this category of material culture to broaden your understanding. As discussed in Chapter 2, it is important to have conducted some secondary reading in preparation for your research project, but at this stage it might be necessary to fill gaps in this knowledge. For example, if you have looked at one or more German stoneware vessels (also referred to as Bellarmine jugs) and consulted any associated documentation, a productive next step is to read about this category of object. A comprehensive treatment of the subject could be found in David Gaimster's *German Stoneware, 1200–1900: Archaeology and cultural history*.[18] This kind of reading will consolidate your understanding of the material evidence conveyed by stoneware artefacts: their methods of manufacture, and the locations and periods in which they were made, traded and consumed. However, it will also introduce you to some of the social and cultural context of these artefacts, which will provide you with potential leads to follow up. For example, once you have got to know these objects materially, then it could be that your research focuses on the trade in these objects throughout early modern Europe. Whilst preparatory reading might have helped you to gain a general picture of this subject area, more specific literature might now be relevant. By starting with the material evidence, you are better able to tailor your broader, contextual reading to best support the focus of your research.

Not all research projects will start with the objects and work outwards, but when they do, the methods of analysis and sequence of research suggested here will serve well. Moreover, for research projects which use objects less centrally, employing some of the methods discussed above will help deepen your analysis of the material artefacts and make sure that the evidence they provide works hard for the argument you wish to make. Wherever you use material culture to help build an historical narrative, considering all the available evidence is key, whether that is evidence observed in person, comparable data from other sources or contextual information garnered from documentary sources or wider reading.

IN SUMMARY

Depending on your research questions, the factors you choose to emphasise may vary, but the logic of moving through a sequence of observable, comparable and supplementary data is helpful and can be concluded by contextualising this data with wider reading on the social, cultural, economic or political world in which your objects operate. Once this process is complete, you will be ready to re-edit or write up your findings into an appropriate format – which is the subject of the next chapter.

NOTES

1 J. D. Prown, 'Mind in Matter: An introduction to material culture theory and method', *Winterthur Portfolio*, 17:1 (1982), 1–19.

2 G. Finley, 'The Gothic Revival and the Victorian Church in New Brunswick: Toward a strategy for material culture research', *Material Culture Review*, 32 (1990), 1–16.

3 R. Batchelor, 'Not Looking at Kettles', in S. Pearce (ed.), *Interpreting Objects and Collections* (London: Routledge, 1994), pp. 139–43.

4 See J. McIntosh, *The Practical Archaeologist: How we know what we know about the past*, 2nd edn (New York: Facts on File, 1999), especially 'Physical Examination', pp. 116–17.

5 These techniques include inductively coupled plasma spectrometry, neutron activation analysis, atomic absorption spectrometry, isotopic analysis and beta-ray backscattering.

6 For more information see A.N. Shugar and J.L. Mass (eds), *Handheld XRF for Art and Archaeology*, Studies in Archaeological Sciences (Leuven: Leuven University Press, 2008).

7 N. Griffiths, A. Jenner and C. Wilson, *Drawing Archaeological Finds: A handbook* (London: Archetype, 1990), p. 9.

8 The Collections Trust have produced this helpful 'how to' guide to the digitisation process: www.collectionstrust.org.uk/images/documents/Digitisation/digitisation_a_simple_guide.pdf [accessed 28 January 2016].

9 See English Heritage, '3D Laser Scanning for Heritage: Advice and guidance to users for laser scanning in archaeology and architecture', 2nd edn (Swindon: English Heritage, 2011), https://historicengland.org.uk/images-books/publications/3d-laser-scanning-heritage2 [accessed 21 September 2016].

10 The British Museum now has a number of 3-D scanned models available to download which are been printed in the museum for use in educational and curatorial projects: www.sketchfab.com/britishmuseum [accessed 7 May 2016].

11 For example, in 3-D images and models, cracks and surface textures that can be difficult to see on the original are sometimes made clearer to the eye. For more on the use of 3-D technology in conservation and curation, see M. Hess, G. Were, I. Brown, S. MacDonald, S. Robson and F. Simon Miller, 'E-Curator: A 3-D web-based archive for conservators and curators', *Ariadne* 60 (2009): www.ariadne.ac.uk/issue60/hess-et-al [accessed 21 January 2016].

12   The exact composition of materials referred to as 'bronze' can actually vary quite widely and may include aluminium, manganese, nickel, zinc and even non-metals such as phosphorus. The exact chemical composition of a 'bronze' object might also give clues to the historical period in which it was made.

13   For example, bronze is used for ship's propellers.

14   On the whole, museums today focus their energies on conservation rather than restoration, being more concerned with arresting deterioration than restoring original appearance.

15   Although this is also a very valuable approach when researching a particular category of artefact, which may reside in many different collections globally.

16   See Figures 5.3–5 and the Metropolitan Museum of Art catalogue: 2009.300.1494a, b; 1973.114.4a, b; 2009.300.1408.

17   For more detail on how to get the most out of object records, see Chapter 4, pp. 98–118.

18   D. Gaimster, *German Stoneware, 1200–1900: Archaeology and cultural history* (London: British Museum,1997).

RECOMMENDED FURTHER READING

Elliot, Robert, et al., 'Towards a Material History Methodology', in S.M. Pearce (ed.), *Interpreting Objects and Collections* (London: Routledge, 1994), pp. 109–24.

McClung Fleming, E., 'Artifact Study: A proposed model', *Winterthur Portfolio* 9 (1974), 153–73.

❧ 6 ❧

WRITING UP FINDINGS

While there are many different ways to present your research – in a seminar presentation, a public talk or a lecture, for example – it is likely that you will also be aiming to create a written piece. There are a wide variety of places where your writing might appear, from blogposts and online exhibitions to academic essays, dissertations and theses. Increasingly university programmes include exercises such as creating a website as formal outcomes of courses. Moreover, such formats of written work are commonly used by professionals working across the fields of academia, public history, museums and heritage.

In this chapter we will focus on the specific elements of writing that relate to material culture-driven historical studies, highlighting the standard conventions of presentation and also techniques that can help engage your reader with objects that can only be reproduced in two dimensions on the page or screen. The chapter will start with a discussion of the practical aspects of incorporating objects within your writing and then move on to provide more specific guidance for different types of writing: essays and dissertations, blogposts, labels and exhibition reviews. Finally, the chapter will advise on publishing your work, highlighting specific issues related to publications using material culture.

MAKING OBJECTS PRESENT IN WRITING

When writing about material culture, you are always aware that the reader is unlikely to be in the presence of the object itself. This, of course, is not the case for a museum label, and these differences will be noted in the section below. The most obvious way of making objects present in your writing is by reproducing images of them. Photographs immediately bring the reader into the world of the object, allowing them to study it for themselves. A photograph also makes it possible to refer in the text to very specific features, demonstrating the detail of your object analysis. Effective use of visual reproductions can help to demonstrate the way that you are thinking through the objects and their centrality to your research and conclusions. You can also consider including images of detailed parts of objects; the two-dimensional limits of the photograph mean there may well be sections which are difficult to see, such as features on the reverse which require an additional illustration.

Including photographic reproductions of objects within your writing might appear straightforward, but it can require careful planning and consideration of practical, financial and legal issues. For an unpublished work – such as an essay, dissertation or thesis – it is unlikely that you will have to pay for the rights of reproduction as outlined below, but you should follow the conventions of presentation and check carefully the permissions and credits associated with images, especially those sourced online. If your thesis later appears online, you should re-check the permissions; it is possible that you will have to remove certain images at this juncture. Extended essays or MA dissertations which you did not plan to publish when you embarked on the project may be suitable for publication further down the line, in which case you will probably have to cut down the number of images and prioritise them carefully for the published version of the work. Further guidance on reproducing photographs in publications is provided below (p. 155–6).

If objects belong to you or your family members, or are found in other non-institutional locations, ensure that any photographs you take during research are of a high enough quality to be reproduced (check journal and publishers' guidelines in advance).[1] It can seriously impede your research and publications if you have to return to research sites to retake photographs at the correct resolution. As noted in Chapter 4, when approaching individuals you should establish that they give their consent for images of their possessions to be reproduced, even if this is for an unpublished piece of writing. One procedure that can help prevent misunderstandings is to create a form for participants to sign (as discussed in Chapter 4, pp. 113–14). This form should not be an intimidating legal document, but it can usefully demonstrate to the individuals with whom you are working how you will be recording and using the material. It is also good practice to verify the wording acceptable to both parties for the captions (e.g. 'Image reproduced courtesy of…'). Ensuring that these terms have been agreed upon shows respect for those who have provided access to material for your research.

Remember that even if you took a photograph, you do not necessarily own the copyright to the image.

For objects and works in museum collections, it is possible that the institution will already have photographs of individual objects, either in online databases or held by the institution itself. In the first instance, where photographs are visible online, most institutions have instructions on their websites explaining how to secure permission to use images and it is worth reading these carefully. Each institution is different, but several allow students and scholars to copy low-resolution images from their websites to use in presentations and unpublished work such as theses, with the correct acknowledgement (see p. 144–5 below).

ILLUSTRATING ABSENT OBJECTS

Given the potential limitations imposed by the various processes out-lined above, it is worth thinking carefully about other options. If funds are limited, some journal and e-book publishers may allow you to add a link to an object's webpage as a footnote, but it is unlikely they will encourage this practice.

Sketching objects is a useful analytical practice (see Chapter 5, pp. 127–8) even if you do not consider yourself a skilled artist. The act of attempting to reproduce the object on a page often raises questions about its materiality, changes in its surface texture, and how it fits together and balances. Such questions can assist with your research practice and they may also be useful adjuncts to your methodology. If you are a confident artist, sketches of objects could usefully stand in for photographs.

Diagrams can enhance your argument, particularly if locations are sig-nificant, or if you wish to discuss the relation between objects in a space (whether a domestic setting, exhibition or museum). As we saw in earlier chapters, the spatial relationship between objects is critical to our under-standing of their meaning. Maps may also be relevant, particularly if you are tracing the biography of an object over a geographical distance.

However, if you are unable to reproduce the object in this way then the writing alone must convey the materiality of the object through care-ful description. Describing objects effectively depends to some extent on your writing style, but taking time to study museum and gallery catalogue descriptions and glossaries of technical terms can enhance the specificity of your writing. These descriptions can be built into your argument, whilst also demonstrating your method of analysis: 'the three spouts on the top of this Ugandan drinking vessel allow for several people to drink from it simultaneously'. This example refers, in fact, to a specific ceremony described in other sources, which again allows you to incorporate the way in which other sources inform, corroborate or challenge your material analysis. Comparisons can also 'bring the object to life'; for example, relating the weight of an object to an everyday activity, the texture on touch, or the awkwardness of moving it. Illumination of such features of an object make it more present to the reader and demonstrates a rigorous approach to studying material culture. However, it is important not to shift into speculation during these physical descriptions; keep them firmly focused on the factual evidence before you. Always ensure that object descriptions remain source-based and are able to help drive forward the argument, or invite interesting challenges to it.

Captions and references

Unlike the standard systems of making reference to text, which have manuals catering for different styles (such as the *Chicago Manual of Style*[2]), there are no standard formats for captions relating to objects, so the format is usually decided either by publishers or authors. Of course, captions explain what an illustration shows but, as with references to written sources, they also allow other scholars to locate these objects. Captions also indicate that permission has been granted to reproduce an image by an institution, if that is relevant. Images, once they are in a text, are referred to as 'figures' and are placed in numerical order. In a more substantial publication, such as a book, it could be that figures are numbered both sequentially and by the chapter they appear in; for example, the second figure in Chapter 4 would appear as 'Figure 4.2'. If you choose this method, images in the Introduction can be numbered using 0: Figure 0.1.

Standard minimum inclusions within the caption are the object name, its maker (if known) or culture from which it comes, its date of production and its accession number. In the case of certain types of objects, such as prints and drawings, there are specific conventions: for example, the title of the work should be italicised. You may also want to include notes such as the materials used and the technique; sometimes these can be combined, such as 'lacquered wood with mother of pearl inlay'. Including the dimensions is highly recommended; when objects are presented in isolation in a book, their scale is entirely lost.

Traditionally, it was not uncommon for historians to use images without these detailed references, but this good practice should be encouraged for those engaged with the study of material things. The captions used throughout this book offer a variety of examples of full captions, which can be used for reference.

Checklist for captions

- figure number
- name/description of object
- maker
- geographical origin
- date of production
- accession number (if from an institution)
- location and/or credit line for institution/photographer

Also consider including:
- materials
- technique
- dimensions

OBJECTS IN HISTORICAL WRITING

Essays and dissertations

There are many guides to the writing of history for students and other writers and we will not replicate these thorough studies here. The first guide in this series, *Using Film as a Source* (2015) by Sian Barber, for example, gives an excellent overview of general matters of form and style in writing history essays, before specifying the particularities of writing about film.[3] The 'Recommended further reading' section at the end of this chapter will provide further references to general guides. If you are writing an extended piece, or even a shorter essay, it is likely to be structured around the following standard elements:

- introduction to research area and questions
- description of sources and methodology
- literature review
- analysis
- conclusion.

These sections relate closely to the project structure outlined in the Introduction on p. 10. As discussed in Chapter 2, clear and rigorous research questions are fundamental to the success of your project. They also form the foundations for how you write up the findings, and make this process less daunting.

Setting out your research questions within the introduction establishes the reason for the project so it is clear to the reader what you plan to achieve and argue. As emphasised throughout this book, material culture presents a particular type of source and making the way in which you engage with it methodologically clear forms a key part of your writing-up. Describing your chosen methodology can be challenging and sources to make this task easier can be found in the 'Further recommended reading' section below; there are also examples of a range of methodologies in Chapter 3. Your discussion of the methodology and the chosen sources offers the main opportunity for you to make clear to the reader (who may not be a material culture specialist) why these sources and this approach allow you to answer your research questions, and perhaps to do so in an innovative way. In essence your methodology should describe how you used your sources to answer your research questions. This superficially simple task actually requires the description of a number of aspects of the project, including:

- which approaches you used and which other scholars' work informed these choices
- where the sources were and how you examined them
- why these methods and approaches are appropriate for answering these research questions
- what new insights these methods can bring.

Before you begin your own writing, it is worth reading several examples of introductions to journal articles or dissertations and thinking about how they are describing their methodology. Unlike some disciplines in the social sciences, where methodology is clearly indicated in a numbered section, in historical writing the methodology is often embedded within a broader introductory section. Nonetheless, reading a number of different works and thinking about the way they described their research process (rather than the historical content) is a good exercise. You can also use these introductory sections to discuss the challenges inherent in piecing together the story of objects and the various absences in the material and archival record. It is worth highlighting the fragmentary nature of the sources and how you dealt with these gaps, as these are methods you used to answer the research questions.

As you write the introductory sections, make sure that you explain how and why you decided upon the particular scale of the project to make your argument. Was there a core body of material you examined in detail? Did you compare these sources with other collections (perhaps online)? There will be both intellectual and practical factors that shaped your study and you should explain the process of defining the limits of the research. Where it is relevant, you should also describe how you integrated the use of archives and other sources with material culture. There is a spectrum of practice within history concerning the degree to which studies clearly articulate the decision-making processes during the research and you will find that some studies do not discuss this topic in much detail at all. However, when conducting research on a non-traditional historical source such as material culture, transparency is a helpful intellectual exercise for the writer. Moreover, a clear explanation of the methodology will help guide the reader through the particularities of this kind of research, which may not be familiar to them, and in doing so help them to judge its value accurately.

Essays and theses do not usually have a limit on the number of photographs permitted (it is only when you decide to publish that you will need to consider the questions of permissions; see pp. 155–6 below for full details), which gives you licence to illustrate your work richly and to include details of objects as well as contextual images. However, it is still worth being critical about those you choose to include by scrutinising what they are doing for your work: Are they contextual (e.g. maps or views, portraits) or are they primary evidence? If they are historical images, it may also be worth discussing the production of the image; as you are a historian attentive to materiality and visual culture, you should treat these images with the same care as you do objects. For images of objects, consider the different angles that illustrate points you are making in the text. Check that you have made reference to all the pictures you include (a quick search through the figure numbers can help); if you do not actually discuss them in the text then they are probably superfluous.

In your conclusion, in addition to reinforcing the central arguments of the piece, you may want to reiterate the value of using material culture to examine your historical period or theme. You can also signal the potential for future lines of research which build on this: it is likely you will not have been able to study every object, every collection or every repository. Emphasise what you were able to achieve within the scope of the essay or dissertation and highlight the future possibilities for a material culture approach to your topic.

Exhibition labels

Increasingly university courses include assessments that are designed to give students a wider range of experiences during their undergraduate and postgraduate careers: experiences that go beyond the exam hall and enhance graduate employability. For example, instead of being asked to write an essay on the meanings of collections in the past or present, a student might instead be asked to stage an exhibition within the university or library, or to create a website or online exhibition. Whilst the amount of written work associated with an exhibition might be less than that for an essay, the words that are used need to be very carefully chosen, as the message of the display has to be conveyed through a combination of media.

The prevailing format for exhibitions is to include some panels of text beside a display, but to always include a label referring to each individual object in the exhibit. In cultural institutions, house style dictates the format of such object labels, including the number of words they use. If you are making an exhibition yourself then you can decide upon the format, but it is worth considering that the limits imposed within the museum profession have been devised for good reasons, not least in terms of the visitor's experience of an exhibition.

Text within exhibitions takes many forms including section titles, text panels and object labels. Exhibitions are usually organised into sections, each of which has a title and usually an introductory panel to a) set out the context and b) explain to the visitor why this selection of objects has been put together. The font size of these different types of text decreases as their quantity increases, so they are often considered as a hierarchy (i.e. panels – larger text, fewer of them; labels – small text, many of them). However, research in museums suggests that labels are often the text the visitor reads first, especially in permanent galleries where introductory panels might be missed as visitors dip in and out of the display. Permanent exhibitions are often telling several different stories, whereas temporary exhibitions usually build a route using structures such as partitions, to ensure the visitor is guided through the displays in a very particular way to follow the narrative.

In both cases, object labels are critical. Guidance varies according to institution but it is common for them to be between fifty and a hundred words. This will seem like a very small amount, especially if you have been researching objects carefully over some time, but consider how much you are asking the visitor to read during an exhibition visit. Keeping labels to around seventy words or fewer responds to the average concentration of museum visitors. Label b in Figure 6.1 has fifty-four words, showing how much you can do with a small amount of text. Longer explanations should be saved for catalogue entries or supporting online exhibitions.

As can be seen in Figure 6.1a, the object label usually consists of the title or the object name (when it is not an artwork this can include a short description), what it is made from and the date and place of origin. In examples 6.1b and 6.1c the material from which these objects were made is described in the object name. The accession number can be placed at the bottom. This brief top-level information is essential for visitors who quickly want to establish what an object is and its basic context. The inclusion of an accession number allows individuals to follow up later if they wish to find out more. Including the title and basic details can save explanatory words in your label. Ultimately a label should help the visitor understand two things: What is it? Why is it here? You cannot say everything about an object; as we have seen throughout this book, objects have long biographies but you will have selected an object to tell a particular story, so you must use the limited space available to explain how the object relates to this particular theme. In the examples above, these ceramic objects related to the history of trade, exchange and movement of material culture in the Indian Ocean. Visitors might be attracted to an object and then read the label, so one measure of 'success' for a label is for the visitor to look *back* at the object after reading the label. There are different ways to achieve this outcome: the label can draw attention to a particular detail they might have missed at first glance (as in Figure 6.1b), or it can explain something about the object's construction or context which makes the visitor look afresh at the object. In Figure 6.1c, the text draws attention to the unusual use of the spoon. If visitors focus back on the object, this suggests that your label has highlighted something new for them to look at, indicating a deeper engagement with the object. If space permits, quotations from the archive can be very powerful for giving a voice to someone from the past who referred to objects of this type or whose words can conjure an image of how they were used.

a	b
Object name/description Material, date and place of production	**b** Porcelain plate featuring VOC ships China, AD 1723–1750
Description (50–100 words)	The VOC (Dutch East India Company) was the major European trading company in the Indian Ocean in the AD 1600s and 1700s. This plate depicts VOC ships moored off Cape Town, with Table Mountain in the distance. Cape Town was founded in 1652 by the VOC. Dutch flags are visible on the hills beyond.
Donor credit if required; Accession number	Donated by A. W. Franks, Franks.599
c Porcelain blue-and-white spoon Fujian, China, AD 1800–1900	
This spoon was found in a grave in Mombasa, Kenya, in AD 1904. By this time, Chinese ceramics had been imported into East Africa for over a thousand years. The collector recorded that such spoons were used in mosques for burning ambergris, a valuable substance found in the digestive system of sperm whales.	
Donated by Sir Claud Hollis, Af1904.-.290	

Figure 6.1 Sample object label format (a) and two examples (b and c)

Online exhibitions allow a greater word count, but it is still good practice not to go over 150 words (or the equivalent of the amount of text you can see on the page at the same time as the photograph of the object).

Blogposts

Academic blogposts are now very common and have become widely recognised as an important way of writing shorter, more experimental reflections on your research. Object-based studies lend themselves well to blogposts as, similarly to an exhibition catalogue, the optimum word-count for an entry is about 1000 words, allowing a particular object or object-type, methodology or collection to be discussed in a medium level of detail. Many scholars regularly read blogs to gain an informal impression of research in the field, and this form of writing offers a legitimate space to test out new ideas and to make public your interest in a particular set of sources or a research area. The use of primary source evidence does not need to be as detailed as it would be in a journal article or book, and indeed one reason for the post might be to share initial findings and to see if colleagues elsewhere can suggest other sources to consult. You do have the space to speculate, as long as you make clear that these are provisional ideas rather than fully formed evidence-based conclusions. You can also add links to other opinion pieces and comparable objects online. However, with blogposts or other more informal pieces, it is worth remembering that they should still be approached rigorously. Any writing to which you put your name reflects on your public profile as a researcher. Although blogposts are not peer-reviewed or physically printed, you should be able to stand by and defend the opinions you state in this format. Furthermore, if you are associating your work with an object in a museum or elsewhere, people who search online for such objects may find your post and, as such, you are adding to the searchable history of that object. Although in scholarly circles blogposts would be treated as 'works in progress', members of the public can perceive them differently. Therefore, it is important to ensure that you note your sources and make clear when you are presenting an opinion rather than a fact.

Examples of useful blogs

- A research project: the East India Company at Home project website included object-based case studies from scholars both in and outside academic institutions: http://blogs.ucl.ac.uk/eicah [accessed 21 September 2016].
- An individual: this blog is written by a curator working in museums but reflecting on wider issues in museums, history and art, including object-based studies, exhibition reviews and discussion of issues in the sector: www.spoonsontrays.com [accessed 15 September 2016].
- A university group: this blog links several departments in University College London: www.materialworldblog.com [accessed 15 September 2016].

Exhibition reviews

Exhibition or gallery reviews involve the examination and discussion of objects in a particular arrangement. In such cases, your opinion and the impressions that the exhibition made upon *you* are relevant as you are making a qualitative judgement about the value and effectiveness of the exhibition. Exhibitions are complex productions to stage and will be the result of months of work by teams of people from conception through to design and installation. Before writing one yourself, you should read reviews in newspapers, blogs and journals to assess different styles of review-writing. For example, some reviewers choose to 'walk' the reader through the exhibition, while others prefer to discuss key objects.

Historians are most likely to review exhibitions around a historical theme rather than, say, those focused on the works of a particular artist, where art historical reviewers will be better placed to judge the quality of the works. A historical approach will usually limit itself to assessing what these objects illuminate about the larger theme, rather than making aesthetic judgements about the quality of the artistry on display. When visiting an exhibition, consider how the ambience of each space is created by the lighting of objects and look closely at how they are displayed as well as the arguments made within the exhibition text. Consider how the arrangement and juxtaposition of objects supports those arguments. Do the sections make an effective sequence or help to tell a particular story? Is the representation fair or have the voices of some relevant people been omitted? Are significant inclusions or exclusions explained?

When writing up a review, you may want to set out the context of the scholarship in brief for the non-expert reader and address questions about why this exhibition is relevant and timely, or how it brings research findings into the public arena. It is important to consider how non-experts might approach the material, but it is also advisable not to underestimate the public's understanding. Consider too the size of the institution, and the scale of funding behind the exhibition and how this might have affected the display; exhibitions and loans are costly endeavours. If you mention how the inclusion of a particular object from another collection could have enhanced the overall effect, be aware that this omission might have been the result of financial or practical constraints rather than an intellectual decision.

If possible, contextualise your own impressions of an exhibition by reading the accompanying exhibition catalogue, as it is in this publication that curators and researchers will set out the intellectual agenda. By fully acknowledging the intentions of the exhibition creators, it will be easier to evaluate whether or not their vision has been effectively realised within the parameters of the space and budget. Judge the exhibition by its own ambitions rather than what you might have preferred or expected to see.

PUBLISHING YOUR WORK

Journal articles and book chapters

For early career researchers, publishing work is essential for establishing an academic career. Making your original contribution to knowledge more widely available is a key part of an academic role. By publishing, you make it possible for other people to be able to refer to and cite your work and see the primary sources you have worked on. Other researchers may subsequently disagree with you, but publishing is the first step to engaging in the academic debate. Even if you do not wish to pursue a career in academia, it is rewarding to publish findings from a dissertation as it puts your work into the public domain for others to use. Journal articles and chapters in edited books are the natural starting point for publishing smaller-scale projects and they are also a good training ground for publishing a book-length study at a later stage. It is important, too, that you choose a topic which lends itself to a piece of writing of this length and also the restrictions of image reproduction. For example, you should not try to condense a thesis of 80,000 words into an article of 7,000 words; it is better practice to choose a compelling example within the thesis, which illustrates your approach and the importance of your material, and signals the originality of the research. Material culture as a source can be helpful in this respect; astute selection of a number of objects (or even one, or one type) can work well in journal articles and book chapters. Edited volumes often emerge from a conference or workshop, in which case you will have already selected material which immediately engages the audience and, with luck, you will also have received feedback.

Journal articles and book chapters are often similar in length (at the time of writing, 6–7,000 words including footnotes is typical although it will depend upon the publisher). There are some key differences between these two forms of writing that we will discuss here and also some features which are similar. For example, both forms will be subject to peer review prior to confirming publication. In the case of edited books, the editors of the book will probably do a first round of reviews and then the whole manuscript will be sent by publishers to external readers – usually, academics in universities with expertise in the area. Articles submitted to a journal will be reviewed by one or more of the editorial board and/or sent to external readers. These processes can take several months, and when you receive feedback the article or chapter is likely to require further editing and sometimes additional research on your part. Revisions of this kind are designed to improve the work and meet the standards expected by the journal or book. Peer-reviewed articles are a highly regarded academic achievement on account of the rigorous process the research goes through, so it is worth putting in the necessary additional time to respond fully to readers' reports.

Although there are no strict rules on writing journal articles and book chapters, consider the different audiences and contexts of these two forms of writing. A journal article which is not part of a special issue (e.g. with a subject-specific title and introduction) will necessarily require a more significant historiographical section setting up the context for your argument. Unless it is a specialist journal, it is likely that the historical context will need explaining alongside the historiographical literature with which you have engaged. As a historian using material culture as a source, it is possible that you are introducing new sources to the field and offering a fresh, or perhaps competing, interpretation of an existing historical question. In this case, it is particularly important that you show a command of the secondary literature and demonstrate clearly the significance of your contribution to the debate and the value of a material culture approach. Avoid using jargon, especially if you are trying to persuade readers of the value of material sources as there may be readers who are sceptical. Making your argument clearly is the most powerful approach.

If you are contributing to a special issue of a journal or an edited book, the theme has already been set out. The issue may have a material culture theme, or you might have been asked to contribute because your work clearly offers a new interpretation of the key themes. In these cases, the introduction by the editors will set out some of the wider historiographical and methodological context so, within your article or chapter, you have more space for analysis and it might be possible to incorporate a wider range of primary material.

These are broad suggestions and journals will differ but it is useful to bear in mind these general differences when considering where to publish your work and how to plan the piece of writing.

When seeking to publish in a journal or a book, it is important to establish early on how many illustrations are permitted so that you can order necessary images well in advance, apply for funds if necessary and shape the article accordingly. For a published work, the quantity of images is in most cases pre-determined by the publisher. Journals vary on the number of pictures they will print; for historical publications (as opposed to art historical) this is usually around four per article of 6,000 words and they tend to be reproduced in black and white. For a chapter in an edited book, you may be able to increase the number if other contributors to the volume have used fewer images. If you wish to present images in colour, this increases the costs of reproduction substantially and you will probably be asked to provide funds for this yourself. Some funding bodies have grants to support the publication of images but it is certainly worth factoring in whether or not you have the time and capacity to make such applications to support the publication.

If you are publishing the image in print or e-book format, most institutions will require you to buy the image rights. For larger archives and museums there is a standard route for you to follow; note that, before making your request, you must ensure that you have the following information from the publishers of the journal or book: estimated print run, UK or worldwide rights, e-book and print copy, resolution required (in dpi). Depending on the institution, each image can cost up to £100 and will have particular legal requirements about the wording of acknowledgements. Often it is necessary to send a copy of the publication to the institution.

It may be the case that the institution does not already have photographs of the objects you wish to illustrate or there is a particular part of the object that is central to your argument which has not yet been photographed. You may personally have taken your photographs on the research visit but, even if so, you should seek out the institution's policy on giving permission to use the image or acknowledge the source in the publication. You can often also request photography of objects from institutions; this will result in high-quality photographs which are in some instances taken in studios with appropriate lighting. However, you must allow plenty of time if you wish to order such images; it can take several weeks or months to arrange depending on the museum's capacity. You will probably have to pay for new photography.

Similarly, if you take photographs of a display within a museum or gallery, you should still check whether you need permission to reproduce the image. With the increasing circulation of digital images online, institutions are reacting differently: some are relaxing their regulations, others tightening them. Taking these various factors into account necessitates careful consideration of which images are most important to your publication and will really enhance the reader's understanding of your work.

Contributions to exhibition catalogues

Another form of published object-focused writing is an exhibition catalogue essay or entry. Exhibition catalogues are published by museums and galleries either in tandem with special exhibitions or to collate information together about a particular set of objects within a collection. These publications can take different forms; nowadays many consist of a series of in-depths essays on themes in an exhibition as well as longer descriptions of individual objects than it is possible to provide in a label. Catalogue entries or essays allow authors to combine objects and discussions in ways which were not possible within the confines of an exhibition where the arrangement of objects is fixed. Cross-referencing is much more acceptable in a publication than in an exhibition which might require a visitor to walk back into another room to examine another object to understand the point being made.

A wide range of scholars might contribute to exhibition catalogues. Object-based catalogue entries usually offer the space to write around 500 words about a single object. Naturally you should take advice on the form and content from the editors of the catalogue but in general the key difference between this kind of writing and an object label is the space that it affords to expand on your observations. For scholars, a key element is explaining where research for these observations came from, therefore contributions need to have full references (unlike labels, which rarely afford the space to cite their sources). If an exhibition catalogue covers a specific artist or historical period, you do not need to repeat material from the introduction, but focus instead on the specific context or archival material that relates to this object. You can refer to objects elsewhere in the catalogue and beyond.

Local history

Local history is an important and vibrant area for publishing accessible historical research relevant for a wide audience focused around a particular geographical region or community. Participating in local history research offers the opportunity to present your work to a receptive audience eager to know more about a specific locality. Local history societies often have their own publications which can take various forms – including guidebooks, pamphlets, journals and blogs.[4] In such publications, the emphasis is often upon the narrative and presenting new evidence about local figures and sites, rather than explaining your theoretical standpoint or methodological framework. You should certainly explain how and where you located your sources and what new findings they reveal, as other local historians may want to follow up these leads.

IN SUMMARY

Reaching the end of a research project which has been conducted and written up in a thoughtful and rigorous way should be satisfying. Here, we have delved into both the detail of historical practice and that of museums and heritage because, inevitably, material culture research will combine knowledge of both. By developing as a researcher who can bridge the concerns of academia and collections-based work, you will be better able to produce material culture research of the highest quality. At the time of writing, the spheres of higher education and heritage institutions are developing ever-closer connections, and effective writing about objects is becoming increasingly central for both.

NOTES

1   See Chapter 5, pp. 129–30, for more details on how to take photographs of objects.
2   University of Chicago Press, *The Chicago Manual of Style*, 16th edn (Chicago: University of Chicago Press, 2010).
3   S. Barber, *Using Film as a Source* (Manchester: Manchester University Press, 2015).
4   See www.local-history.co.uk/Groups [accessed 24 May 2016] for a list of local history societies, whose individual websites give information about publications and blogs.

RECOMMENDED FURTHER READING

Australian Museum, *Writing Text and Labels*: www.australianmuseum. net.au/writing-text-and-labels [accessed 29 January 2016].
Barber, Sian, *Using Film as a Source* (Manchester: Manchester University Press, 2015).
Barnet, Sylvan, *A Short Guide to Writing about Art*, 9th edn (Boston, MA: Pearson/Prentice Hall, 2011), pp. 157–74 (Chapter 7: 'Writing a review of an exhibition').
Black, Jeremy, and Donald. M. MacRaild, *Studying History*, 3rd edn (Basingstoke: Palgrave Macmillan, 2007).
Kalfatovic, Martin R., *Creating a Winning Online Exhibition: A guide for libraries, archives and museums* (London and Chicago, IL: Hodder & Stoughton, 2002).

AFTERWORD

This guide has sought to show that material culture is a valuable and accessible source of evidence for historians and one that can prompt new ways of thinking about the past. As we have seen, material culture articulates relationships and interactions between people, things, and broader societal structures and networks. By combining examples of this kind of scholarship with details of how a researcher can access objects to study, we hope to have demystified the practice of material culture history and made it more approachable for the reader. The guide opened with chapters that described the reasons why historians might be drawn to material culture as a primary source and also the range of other disciplines that have developed theoretical and methodological expertise in thinking about 'things'. We then moved on to discuss the importance of detailed project planning and careful use of available resources to locate evidence relevant to answering research questions. Primary sources are necessarily combined with methods of analysis and an over-arching methodology, which we viewed through the lens of existing historical studies. Finally, guidance was provided on the ways in which you might document, analyse and 'write up' research findings. Whilst this guidance is not exhaustive, it provides a firm basis for researchers of all kinds to undertake effective work in this field.

Material culture history is a growing and vibrant field of research and one which increasingly influences currents of debate within the wider discipline. In response, undergraduate courses in history have started to include modules or seminars on how to use material culture as a source. Moreover, historical research on material culture has led to significant shifts both intellectually and in terms of how the practice of academic history is understood. Traditionally, academic research and public engagement remained largely separate enterprises, universities being the home of the former whilst cultural organisations took up the work of the latter. In recent decades, however, university-based historians have chosen to engage with museums and heritage sites, and their collections, in much greater numbers, a development that reflects fundamental changes in the relationship between academia and the wider world. For example, within university history departments there is a growing emphasis on researching and teaching 'public history'. The practice of public history involves recognising the importance of engaging a diverse range of individuals and communities in the production of history. Of course, curators and practitioners in museums and heritage environments have always been public historians, but closer working relationships between professionals in universities and the cultural sector can only improve the historical work that we do. The effective use of objects remains central to this.

As historians are choosing to engage with material culture in greater numbers than ever before, many come to this field from a training that has strongly prioritised textual evidence. As such, historians have looked outwards to draw on the methods and concepts of neighbouring fields of scholarship, but we have also looked inward – thinking carefully through our own approaches to researching and writing history. In this dynamic arena of new ways of working and thinking, established researchers might be struggling with many of the same difficulties as newcomers to historical enquiry. It is also worth emphasising that new researchers in history are key to this ongoing process of change and will be the ones to take material culture history forward in the long term.

One of the most promising avenues for further exploration comes from research that allies material culture and space, building on the work of historical geographers and thinking about material environments in a holistic way. There are also areas of historical research, such as political history, that have not yet engaged fully with material culture as a primary source, which offers exciting opportunities in the coming years. Study of diplomatic gifts and the performance of political encounters, for example, offers potential for exploration of the materiality of political relationships. Furthermore, as an interdisciplinary endeavour, material culture research invites collaboration between researchers of different disciplines and between researchers and practitioners in museums and heritage settings. By drawing historians out of well-trodden paths and offering connections with alternative ways of thinking, material culture research has the potential to transform our understanding of the past.

Alongside interaction between the disciplines and a creative disruption to traditional patterns of enquiry, another important development has emerged. By bringing material culture into the foreground, historians have been able to engage in a process of democratisation – in terms of both the topics studied and the wider participation of people outside of the academy in the work of history. As we have discussed, material culture can offer a voice to those whose lives have not been recorded in text. However, the broader access to museum collections brought by digitisation and other initiatives has also transformed the accessibility of the histories these objects can tell and invited wider participation in that project. As museum professionals tell us, objects offer an 'approachable' starting point for thinking about the past, inviting engagement with eyes, hands and voice. This remains just as true in the classroom as it does in the gallery. In this way, collections hold the power to attract a diverse population of students to the study of history, requiring a different repertoire of analysis that is not forged in (culturally) specific forms of text and language.

So, what does this growing interest in material culture mean for history – the questions historians ask of the past and the answers we are able to provide? Whilst it is hard to predict what the future might hold, in the present it is clear that a concern with material culture and materiality has promoted an interest in the 'experiential'. What did the past feel like, smell like, taste like? How can tactile engagements with artefacts, materials or processes of making help us to understand these objects, materials and processes in the past? How can we understand the emotional lives of historical actors? How can we conceptualise emotions in the past? The study of these questions through material culture has moved the experiential from a matter of curiosity, previously only brought to the fore during visits to heritage sites, to a fully integrated and respected part of mainstream history.

The study of the experiential is only one of a number of exciting ways ahead. Material culture only seems likely to become more significant to historical study while technological developments continue to expand the toolkit available to historians. As discussed in this book, the ways in which we can record, visualise and analyse individual objects have been revolutionised by the advent of new technologies such as photogrammetry. The accessibility and capabilities of these technologies are increasing in tandem, transforming lab-based science into portable tools for everyday use. Our digital technologies and data management systems are also making unprecedented numbers of objects available to the researcher and presenting opportunities to make and map networks of connections that were previously invisible.

So, what will material culture history look like in the future? Rather than pursuing a path that sees material culture as a 'new' primary source that can be slotted neatly into the super-structure of historical scholarship, we could see objects as more than that. If we were able, as a discipline, to view material culture not only as a form of evidence but also as a way of thinking about the past, then exciting avenues will open up before us. Material culture can play many different roles in our studies of the past, but to make the most interesting leaps of imagination we will need to take the time to see where objects can lead us – allowing them to reveal the past in three dimensions and in ways we cannot yet predict. In training ourselves to study material culture we can develop new repertoires of connection with our twenty-first-century environment and, by doing so, begin to unlock the material world of centuries past.

SELECT BIBLIOGRAPHY AND RESOURCES

BOOKS

Appadurai, A. (ed.), *The Social Life of Things: Commodities in cultural perspective* (Cambridge: Cambridge University Press, 1986).

Attfield, J., *Wild Things: The material culture of everyday life* (Oxford: Berg, 2000).

Barber, S., *Using Film as a Source* (Manchester: Manchester University Press, 2015).

Barnet, S., *A Short Guide to Writing about Art*, 9th edn (Boston, MA: Pearson/ Prentice Hall, 2011).

Barringer, T. J., and T. Flynn (eds), *Colonialism and the Object: Empire, material culture and the museum* (London: Routledge, 1998).

Bennett, T., and P. Joyce (eds), *Material Powers: Cultural studies, history and the material turn* (London: Routledge, 2010).

Black, J., and D. M. MacRaild, *Studying History*, 3rd edn (London: Palgrave Macmillan, 2007).

Bleichmar, D., and P. C. Mancall (eds), *Collecting across Cultures: Material exchanges in the early modern Atlantic world* (Philadelphia, PA: University of Pennsylvania Press, 2011).

Bourdieu, P., *Outline of a Theory of Practice* (Cambridge: Cambridge University Press, 1977).

Brauner, D. R. (ed.), *Approaches to Material Culture Research for Historical Archaeologists*, 2nd edn (Tuscon, AZ: Society for Historical Archaeology, 2000).

Buchli, V. (ed.), *The Material Culture Reader* (Oxford and New York: Berg, 2002).

Byrne, S., A. Clarke and R. Harrison (eds), *Unpacking the Collection: Networks of material and social agency in the museum* (n.p.: Springer, 2012).

Candlin, F., and R. Guins (eds), *The Object Reader* (New York: Routledge, 2009).

Clifford, H., *Silver in London: The Parker and Wakelin partnership, 1760–1776* (London: Yale University Press, 2012).

Cohen, D., *Household Gods: The British and their possessions* (New Haven, CT, and London: Yale University Press, 2006).

Coombes, A. E., *Reinventing Africa: Museums, material culture and popular imagination in late Victorian and Edwardian England* (London: Yale University Press, 1994).

Daston, L. (ed.), *Things that Talk: Object lessons from art and science* (New York: Zone Books, 2004).

Drower, M. S., *Flinders Petrie: A life in archaeology* (London: Gollancz, 1985).

Dudley, S. (ed.), *Museum Objects: Experiencing the properties of things* (London: Routledge, 2012).

Earle, P., *The Making of the English Middle Class: Business, society and family life in London, 1660–1730* (London: Methuen, 1989).

Edwards, E., and J. Hart (eds), *Photographs Objects Histories: On the materiality of images* (London and New York: Routledge, 2004).

Edwards, E., C. Gosden and R. B. Phillips (eds), *Sensible Objects: Colonialism, museums and material culture* (Oxford: Berg, 2006).

Elsner, J., and R. Cardinal (eds), *The Cultures of Collecting* (London: Reaktion, 1994).

Eriksen, T. H., and F. S. Nielsen, *A History of Anthropology* (London: Pluto Press, 2001).

Findlen, P. (ed.), *Early Modern Things: Objects and their histories, 1500–1800* (New York: Routledge, 2012).

Findlen, P., *Possessing Nature: Museums, collecting, and scientific culture in early modern Italy* (Berkeley, CA, and London: University of California Press, 1994).

Foster, J., and J. Sheppard (eds), *British Archives: A guide to archive resources in the United Kingdom* (London: Palgrave, 2002).

Gane, M. (ed.), *The Radical Sociology of Durkheim and Mauss* (London: Routledge, 1992).

Gerritsen, A., and G. Riello (eds), *The Global Lives of Things: The material culture of connections in the early modern world* (London and New York: Routledge, 2016).

Gerritsen, A., and G. Riello (eds), *Writing Material Culture History* (London: Bloomsbury, 2015).

Gosden, C., and C. Knowles, *Collecting Colonialism: Material culture and colonial change* (Oxford: Berg, 2001).

Gosden, C., and F. Larson, *Knowing Things: Exploring the collections at the Pitt Rivers Museum, 1884–1945* (Oxford: Oxford University Press, 2007).

Greig, H., J. Hamlett and L. Hannan (eds), *Gender and Material Culture in Britain since 1600* (London: Palgrave Macmillan, 2015).

Griffiths, N., A. Jenner and C. Wilson, *Drawing Archaeological Finds: A handbook* (London: Archetype, 1990).

Gunn, S., and L. Faire (eds), *Research Methods for History* (Edinburgh: Edinburgh University Press, 2011).

Hamlett, J., *Material Relations: Domestic interiors and middle-class families in England, 1850–1910* (Manchester: Manchester University Press, 2010).

Hamling, T., and C. Richardson (eds), *Everyday Objects: Medieval and early modern material culture and its meanings* (Farnham: Ashgate, 2010).

Harman, G., *Tool-Being: Heidegger and the metaphysics of objects* (Chicago, IL: Open Court, 2002).

Harvey, K. (ed.), *History and Material Culture: A student's guide to approaching alternative sources* (London: Routledge, 2009).

Hatt, M., and C. Klonk, *Art History: A critical introduction to its methods* (Manchester: Manchester University Press, 1996).

Hicks, D., and M. C. Beaudry (eds), *The Oxford Handbook of Material Culture Studies* (Oxford: Oxford University Press, 2010).

Hudson, P., *History by Numbers: An introduction to quantitative approaches* (London: Arnold, 2000).

Huntsman, P., *Thinking about Art: A thematic guide to art history* (Chichester: Wiley-Blackwell, 2015).

Jasanoff, M., *Edge of Empire: Conquest and collecting in the east, 1750–1850* (London: Fourth Estate, 2005).

Jones, A., and P. Stallybrass (eds), *Renaissance Clothing and the Materials of Memory* (Cambridge: Cambridge University Press, 2000).

Jordanova, L., *History in Practice*, 2nd edn (London: Bloomsbury, 2006).

Jordanova, L., *The Look of the Past: Visual and material evidence in historical practice* (Cambridge: Cambridge University Press, 2012).

Kalfatovic, M. R., *Creating a Winning Online Exhibition: A guide for libraries, archives and museums* (Chicago, IL, and London: Hodder & Stoughton, 2002).

Kaplan, F. E. S. (ed.), *Museums and the Making of 'Ourselves': The role of objects in national identity* (London: Leicester University Press, 1994).

Karp, I., and S. D. Lavine (eds), *Exhibiting Cultures: The poetics and politics of museum display* (Washington, DC: Smithsonian Institution Press, 1991).

Kavanagh, G. (ed.), *Museum Languages: Objects and texts* (Leicester: Leicester University Press, 1991).

Kingery, W. D. (ed.), *Learning from Things: Method and theory of material culture studies* (Washington, DC; London: Smithsonian Institution Press, 1996).

Kuklick, H. (ed.), *The New History of Anthropology* (Oxford: Blackwell, 2008).

Latour, B., *Reassembling the Social: An introduction to actor-network-theory* (Oxford: Oxford University Press, 2005).

Latour, B., and S. Woolgar, *Laboratory Life: The social construction of scientific facts* (London: Sage Publications, 1979).

Lawrence, D., *Genteel Women: Empire and domestic material culture, 1840–1910* (Manchester: Manchester University Press, 2012).

Lubar, S. D, and W. D. Kingery (eds), *History from Things: Essays on material culture* (Washington, DC; London: Smithsonian Institution Press, 1993).

MacDonald, S. (ed.), *The Politics of Display: Museums, science, culture* (London: Routledge, 1998).

MacGregor, N., *A History of the World in 100 Objects* (London: Allen Lane, 2010).

Marx, K., *Das Kapital: Kritik der politischen Ökonomie* [*Capital: Critique of political economy*], vols 1–3 (Hamburg: Otto Meissner, 1867).

Mauss, M., *The Gift: The form and reason for exchange in archaic societies* (London: Routledge, 2002).

McIntosh, J., *The Practical Archaeologist: How we know what we know about the past*, 2nd edn (New York: Facts on File, 1999).

Mida, I., and A. Kim, *The Dress Detective: A practical guide to object-based research in fashion* (London: Bloomsbury, 2015).

Miller, D. (ed.), *Acknowledging Consumption: A review of new studies* (London: Routledge, 1995).

Miller, D. (ed.), *Material Cultures: Why some things matter* (London: UCL Press, 1997).

Myers, F. R., *The Empire of Things: Regimes of value and material culture* (Santa Fe, NM: School of American Research Press, 2002).

Pearce, S. M. (ed.), *Interpreting Objects and Collections* (London: Routledge, 1994).

Pearce, S. M. (ed.), *Museums and the Appropriation of Culture* (London: Athlone Press, 1994).

Pearce, S. M. (ed.), *Museum Studies in Material Culture* (Leicester: Leicester University Press, 1989).

Riello, G., *Cotton: The fabric that made the modern world* (Cambridge: Cambridge University Press, 2013).

Riello, G., and T. Roy (eds), *How India Clothed the World: The world of south Asian textiles, 1500–1850* (Leiden: Brill, 2009).

Rose, G., *Visual Methodologies: An introduction to the interpretation of visual materials* (London: Sage, 2007).

Sandell, R. (ed.), *Museums, Society, Inequality* (London: Routledge, 2002).

Shammas, C., *The Pre-Industrial Consumer in England and America* (Oxford: Clarendon, 1990).

Shugar, A. N., and J. L. Mass (eds), *Handheld XRF for Art and Archaeology* (Leuven: Leuven University Press, 2008).

Sloan, K., and A. Burnett (eds), *Enlightenment: Discovering the World in the Eighteenth Century* (London: British Museum Press, 2005).

Snodin, M., and J. Styles, *Design and the Decorative Arts: Britain 1500–1900* (London: V&A, 2001).

Stocking, G. W. (ed.), *Objects and Others: Essays on Museums and Material Culture* (Madison, WI: University of Wisconsin Press, 1985).

Styles, J., and A. Vickery (eds), *Gender, Taste and Material Culture in Britain and North America* (London: The Paul Mellon Centre for Studies in British Art, 2006).

Thomas, N., *Entangled Objects: Exchange, material culture, and colonialism in the Pacific* (Cambridge, MA, and London: Harvard University Press, 1991).

Thompson, J. M., and D. A. Bassett, *A Manual of Curatorship: A guide to museum practice*, 2nd edn (Oxford and Boston, MA: Butterworth-Heinemann, 1992).

Tilley, C. (ed.), *Reading Material Culture: Structuralism, hermeneutics and post-structuralism* (Oxford: Basil Blackwell, 1990).

Tilley, C., W. Keane, S. Kuechler-Fogden, M. Rowlands and P. Spyer (eds), *Handbook of Material Culture* (London and Thousand Oaks, CA: Sage, 2013).

Tosh, J., *The Pursuit of History: Aims, methods and new directions in the study of history*, 6th edn (London: Routledge, 2015).

Turkle, S. (ed.), *Evocative Objects: Things we think with* (Cambridge, MA, and London: MIT Press, 2007).

Ulrich, L. T., S. A. Carter, I. Gaskell, S. Schechner and S. van Gerbig, *Tangible Things: Making history through objects* (Oxford and New York: Oxford University Press, 2015).

Weatherill, L., *Consumer Behaviour and Material Culture in Britain, 1660–1760* (London: Economic and Social Research Council, 1985).

Woodward, I., *Understanding Material Culture* (London: Sage, 2007).

CHAPTERS IN EDITED VOLUMES

Adamson, G., and G. Riello, 'Global Objects: Intention and entanglement', in M. Berg (ed.), *Writing the History of the Global* (Oxford: Oxford University Press and the British Academy, 2013), pp. 177–93.

Akin, M., 'Passionate Possession: The formation of private collections', in W. D. Kingery (ed.), *Learning from Things: Method and theory of material culture studies* (Washington, DC, and London: Smithsonian Institution Press, 1996), pp. 102–28.

Brown, I. W., 'The New England Cemetery as a Cultural Landscape', in S. D. Lubar and W. D. Kingery (eds), *History from Things: Essays on material culture* (Washington, DC: Smithsonian Institution Press, 1993), pp. 140–59.

Elliot, R., et al., 'Towards a Material History Methodology', in S. M. Pearce (ed.), *Interpreting Objects and Collections* (London: Routledge, 1994), pp. 109–24.

Gerritsen, A., 'Ceramics for Local and Global Markets: Jingdezhen's agora of technologies', in D. Schafer and F. Bray (eds), *Cultures of Knowledge: Technology in Chinese history* (Leiden: Brill, 2011), pp. 164–86.

Kopytoff, I., 'The Cultural Biography of Things: Commoditization as process', in A. Appadurai (ed.), *The Social Life of Things: Commodities in cultural perspective* (Cambridge: Cambridge University Press, 1986), pp. 64–91.

Prown, J., 'The Truth of Material Culture: History or fiction?', in S. D. Lubar and W. D. Kingery (eds), *History from Things: Essays on material culture* (Washington, DC: Smithsonian Institution Press, 1993), pp. 1–19.

Richmond, V., 'Stitching the Self: Eliza Kenniff's drawers and the materialization of identity in late-nineteenth-century London', in M. Goggin and B. Fowkes Tobin (eds), *Women and Things: Gendered material strategies, 1750–1950* (Farnham: Ashgate, 2009), pp. 43–54.

Riello, G., '"Things Seen and Unseen": The material culture of early modern inventories and their representation of domestic interiors', in Paula Findlen (ed.), *Early Modern Things: Objects and their histories, 1500–1800* (London: Routledge, 2013), pp. 125–50.

Schaffer, S., 'A Science whose Bubble is Bursting: Soap bubbles as commodities in classical physics', in L. Daston (ed.), *Things that Talk: Object lessons from art and science* (New York: Zone Books, 2004), pp. 147–92.

Senos, N., 'The Empire in the Duke's Palace: Global material culture in sixteenth-century Portugal', in A. Gerritsen and G. Riello (eds), *The*

Global Lives of Things: The material culture of connections in the early modern world (London: Routledge, 2016), pp. 128–44.

Smith, H., 'Gender and Material Culture in the Early Modern London Guilds', in H. Greig, J. Hamlett and L. Hannan (eds), *Gender and Material Culture in Britain since 1600* (London: Palgrave, 2015), pp. 16–31.

JOURNAL ARTICLES

Alberti, S. J. M. M., 'Objects and the Museum', *Isis* 96:4 (2005), 559–71.

Auslander, L., 'Beyond Words', *American Historical Review* 110:4 (2005), 1015–45.

Brown, B., 'Thing Theory', *Critical Enquiry* 28:1 (2001), 1–22.

Finley, G., 'The Gothic Revival and the Victorian Church in New Brunswick: Toward a Strategy for Material Culture Research', *Material Culture Bulletin* 32 (1990), 1–16.

Gosden, C., and Y. Marshall, 'The Cultural Biography of Objects', *World Archaeology* 31:2 (1999), 169–78.

Green, H., 'Cultural History and the Material(s) Turn', *Cultural History* 1:1 (April 2012), 61–82.

Houlbrook, M., 'The Man with the Powder Puff in Interwar London', *Historical Journal* 50:1 (2007), 145–71.

Keating, J., and L. Markey, 'Introduction: Captured objects. Inventories of early modern collections', *Journal of the History of Collections* 23:2 (2011), 209–13.

Longair, S., '"A Grand Show" for East Africa: The Zanzibar Exhibition of 1905', *exPLUSultra* 3 (2012), 1–19.

Martin, M., and D. Bleichmar, 'Introduction: Objects in motion in the early modern world', *Art History* 38:4 (September 2015), 604–19.

McClung Fleming, E., 'Artifact Study: A proposed model', *Winterthur Portfolio* 9 (1974), 153–73.

Miller, D., 'Consumption and Commodities', *Annual Review of Anthropology* 24 (1995), 141–61.

Modest, W., 'We Have always Been Modern: Museums, collections, and modernity in the Caribbean', *Museum Anthropology* 35:1 (2012), 85–96.

Prown, J. D., 'Mind in Matter: An introduction to material culture theory and method', *The Winterthur Portfolio* 17:1 (1982), 1–19.

Schlereth, T. J., 'Material Culture Research and Historical Explanation', *The Public Historian* 7:4 (1985), 21–36.

Styles, J., 'Product Innovation in Early Modern London', *Past & Present* 168:1 (2000), 124–69.

Trentmann, F., 'Materiality in the Future of History: Things, practices, and politics', *Journal of British Studies* 48:2 (2009), 283–307.

ONLINE ARTICLES

Australian Museum, *Writing Text and Labels*: www.australianmuseum.net.au/writing-text-and-labels [accessed 29 January 2016].

Bounia, A., 'Codes of Ethics and Museum Research': *Journal of Conservation and Museum Studies* 12:1 (2014), www.jcms-journal.com/articles/10.5334/jcms.1021214 [accessed 28 January 2016].

The Collections Trust digitisation guide: www.collectionstrust.org.uk/images/documents/Digitisation/digitisation_a_simple_guide.pdf [accessed 28 January 2016].

The Collections Trust guide to catalogues: www.collectionstrust.org.uk/media/documents/c1/a216/f6/CataloguingFactsheet.pdf [accessed 28 January 2016].

East India Company at Home project, including object case studies: http://blogs.ucl.ac.uk/eicah [accessed 19 January 2016].

English Heritage, *3D Laser Scanning for Heritage: Advice and guidance to users for laser scanning in archaeology and architecture*, 2nd edn (Swindon: English Heritage, 2011): https://historicengland.org.uk/images-books/publications/3d-laser-scanning-heritage2 [accessed 21 September 2016].

Gerritsen, A., 'The Global Life of a Soya Bottle', an inaugural lecture at the University of Leiden, 12 December 2014: https://openaccess.leiden-univ.nl/bitstream/handle/1887/32170/Oratie%20Gerritsen.pdf?sequence=1 [accessed 28 January 2016].

Hess, M., G. Were, I. Brown, S. MacDonald, S. Robson and F. Simon Miller, 'E-Curator: A 3-D web-based archive for conservators and curators', *Ariadne* 60 (2009): www.ariadne.ac.uk/issue60/hess-et-al [accessed 21 January 2016].

ICOM guidance on registering objects: http://network.icom.museum/fileadmin/user_upload/minisites/cidoc/DocStandards/CIDOC_Fact_Sheet_No_1.pdf [accessed 28 January 2016].

ICOM guidance on numbering and marking objects: http://icom.museum/fileadmin/user_upload/pdf/Guidelines/CIDOC_Fact_Sheet_No2.pdf [accessed 28 January 2016].

Manias, C., 'Feature Archive: A guide to using museum archives': www. frenchhistorysociety.co.uk/blog/?p=437 [accessed 1 July 2015].

Museums Association, 'Policy and Advocacy', *Annual Report 2015*, p. 10: www.museumsassociation.org/download?id=1151014 [accessed 14 October 2015].

RESOURCES

This is by no means an exhaustive list, but it does give a range of collections (both in terms of subject matter and region) that provide good online access to their catalogues and object images. This list is always growing, but the following examples will provide a starting point for material culture researchers. Most of the examples are collections primarily of objects, but two major national sources for archival material have also been included: the British Library and The National Archives.

Ashmolean Museum
Beaumont Street, Oxford OX1 2PH
+44 (0)1865 278000
www.ashmolean.org
Art and archaeology collections from across the world, from the Palaeolithic era to contemporary art works. Founded originally in 1683, the Ashmolean Museum of Art and Archaeology in its current form was formed in 1908 when the original Ashmolean and the University Art Collection were combined. Collection database: www.ashmolean.org/collections/online [accessed 19 September 2016].

Beamish, the living museum of the north
Regional Resource Centre, Beamish, County Durham DH9 0RG
+44 (0)191 370 4000, museum@beamish.org.uk
www.beamish.org.uk
Open-air museum founded in 1970 representing the social history of the north-east of England, in particular objects, archives and photographs associated with everyday life during the boom of industrial activity in the region in the nineteenth and twentieth centuries. Collection database: http://collections.beamish.org.uk [accessed 19 September 2016].

British Library
96 Euston Road, London NW1 2DB
+44 (0)1937 546060, Customer-Services@bl.uk
www.bl.uk
National library of the United Kingdom, copyright library for books produced in the UK and Northern Ireland. It includes historic book collections as well as official documents and special collections, such as manuscripts and maps. It was originally part of the British Museum until the institutions were separated in 1973.
Library catalogue: http://explore.bl.uk/primo_library/libweb/action/search.do?dscnt=1&dstmp=1455104324970&vid=BLVU1&fromLogin=true [accessed 19 September 2016].

British Museum
Great Russell Street, London WC1B 3DG
+44 (0)20 7323 8299, information@britishmuseum.org
www.britishmuseum.org
Founded in 1753, the British Museum is the largest museum in the UK, with world collections ranging from hand-axes created 2 million years ago to artefacts from the present day, including archaeological and anthropological material, decorative arts, coins, medals and the national collection of prints and drawings. It houses around 8 million objects as well as photographs and documents relating to the collections.
Collection database: www.britishmuseum.org/research/publications/online_research_catalogues.aspx [accessed 19 September 2016].

Europeana project
Online research portal bringing together databases from institutions across Europe enabling the user to search through nearly 50 million objects.
Project portal: www.europeana.eu/portal [accessed 19 September 2016].

Historic England
1 Waterhouse Square, 138–142 Holborn, London EC1N 2ST
+44 (0)20 7973 3700, customers@HistoricEngland.org.uk
www.historicengland.org.uk
Government body responsible for caring for the historic environment and heritage in England. It also has significant archival collections.
Archive database: http://archive.historicengland.org.uk [accessed 19 September 2016].

Lewis Walpole Library (USA)
154 Main Street, Farmington, CT
(mailing address: PO Box 1408, Farmington, CT 06034, USA) + 1 (860) 677-2140, walpole@yale.edu
www.library.yale.edu/walpole
Research centre for eighteenth-century studies, in particular for the study of Horace Walpole and Strawberry Hill. Its collections include important holdings of eighteenth-century British prints, drawings, manuscripts, rare books, paintings and decorative arts.
Collection database: www.library.yale.edu/walpole/collections/digital_collection.html [accessed 19 September 2016].

The Manchester Museum
The University of Manchester, Oxford Road, Manchester M13 9PL
+44 (0)161 275 2634, museum@manchester.ac.uk
www.manchester.ac.uk/museum
Part of the University of Manchester and opened to the public in 1890, this museum has collections of archaeology, anthropology and natural history, and over six million objects.
Collection database: http://harbour.man.ac.uk/mmcustom/narratives [accessed 19 September 2016].

Museum of London
150 London Wall, London EC2Y 5HN
+44 (0)20 7001 9844, info@museumoflondon.org.uk
www.museumoflondon.org.uk
The Museum of London opened in 1976 amalgamated from two older museums – the Guildhall Museum and the London Museum. It has archaeological collections as well as objects related to social and urban history of London. It now has two museum sites: one in the City of London and the Museum of the London Docklands.
Collection database: http://collections.museumoflondon.org.uk/online [accessed 19 September 2016].

The National Archives
The National Archives, Kew, Richmond, Surrey, TW9 4DU
+44 (0)20 8876 3444
www.nationalarchives.gov.uk
Combining the formerly separate departments of the Public Record Office and the Historic Manuscripts Commission, the National Archives house the

official government archives. The collection contains over 11 million historical government and public records, from the Domesday Book to modern
government papers and digital files, as well as paper and parchment,
digital records and websites, photographs, posters, maps, drawings and
paintings.
Archive catalogue: http://discovery.nationalarchives.gov.uk [accessed 19
September 2016].

National Gallery
Trafalgar Square, London WC2N 5DN
+44 (0)20 7747 2885, information@ng-london.org.uk
www.nationalgallery.org.uk
Founded in 1824, the National Gallery houses the national collection of
paintings in the Western European tradition from the thirteenth to the
nineteenth centuries.
Painting catalogue: www.nationalgallery.org.uk/paintings/research/the-na
tional-gallery-catalogues [accessed 19 September 2016].
Search by artist: www.nationalgallery.org.uk/view-the-collection [accessed
19 September 2016].

National Museums of Scotland
Chambers Street, Edinburgh EH1 1JF
+44 (0)300 123 6789, info@nms.ac.uk
www.nms.ac.uk
The National Museums of Scotland encompass four sites: the National
Museum of Scotland, the National War Museum, the National Museum
of Flight and the National Museum of Rural Life. Its collections consist
of objects related to Scottish history as well as items from across the world
including the applied arts, archaeological and anthropological material,
science, technology and natural history collections.
Collection   database: www.nms.ac.uk/explore/search-our-collections
[accessed 19 September 2016].
National Museums Collections Centre:
www.nms.ac.uk/about-us/research/research-facilities/national-muse
ums-collection-centre [accessed 19 September 2016].

National Museum Wales / Amgueddfa Cymru
www.museumwales.ac.uk
See www.museumwales.ac.uk/enquiries for correspondence and contacts
for different museums.

National Museum Wales / Amgueddfa Cymru comprises seven museums across Wales from the National Museum Cardiff (with art, geology and natural history collections), to the St Fagan's National History Museum and the Big Pit National Coal Museum.

Art collection database: www.museumwales.ac.uk/art/online [accessed 19 September 2016].

Library and archive catalogue: www.museumwales.ac.uk/curatorial/library [accessed 19 September 2016].

National Portrait Gallery

St Martin's Place, London WC2H 0HE

+44 (0)20 7306 0055, collection enquiries: archiveenquiry@npg.org.uk

www.npg.org.uk

Founded in 1856 to collect portraits of famous British men and women. Its online database now has around 200,000 portraits from the sixteenth century to the present day.

Collection database: www.npg.org.uk/collections/collection-catalogues.php [accessed 19 September 2016].

National Trust

PO Box 574, Manvers, Rotherham, S63 3FH

+44 (0)344 800 1895, enquiries@nationaltrust.org.uk

www.nationaltrust.org.uk

Founded in 1895 as a charity, the National Trust protects and opens to the public over 350 historic houses, gardens and ancient monuments, as well as forests, moorland, islands, archaeological remains, castles, nature reserves and villages.

Collection database: www.nationaltrustcollections.org.uk [accessed 19 September 2016].

Pitt Rivers Museum

South Parks Road, Oxford OX1 3PP

+44 (0)1865 270927, prm@prm.ox.ac.uk

www.prm.ox.ac.uk

General Augustus Lane-Fox Pitt-Rivers gave his collections to the University of Oxford in 1884. The museum has over 500,000 objects of archaeological and anthropological material from across the world from a wide range of time periods. It is famous for its 'typological' display, which combines objects by type from various cultures together (rather than all objects from a single culture together).

Collection database: www.prm.ox.ac.uk/databases.html [accessed 19 September 2016].

Royal College of Surgeons of England, Hunterian Museum
35–43 Lincoln's Inn Fields, Lincoln's Inn Fields, London WC2A 3PE
+44 (0)20 7405 3474
www.rcseng.ac.uk/museums/hunterian
The Hunterian Museum collections include human and non-human anatomical and pathological specimens, models, instruments, painting and sculpture, relating to the art and science of surgery from the seventeenth century to the present day.
Collection database: http://surgicat.rcseng.ac.uk [accessed 19 September 2016].

Sainsbury Centre for Visual Arts
University of East Anglia, Norwich NR4 7TJ
+44 (0)1603 593 199
www.scva.ac.uk
Through major gifts of the Sainsbury family and other donors, the SCVA has art works from across the world spanning over 5,000 years of history. In addition to important collections of art from Africa, Oceania, the Americas and Asia, and ancient Mediterranean cultures, it also has a significant number of works of twentieth-century European art.
Collection database: www.scva.ac.uk/about/collections [accessed 19 September 2016].

Victoria and Albert Museum
Cromwell Road, London SW7 2RL
+44 (0)20 7942 2000, contact@vam.ac.uk
www.vam.ac.uk
A museum of art and design, the V&A collections cover around 2,000 years of history with objects from across the world. The institution was established in 1852, in the wake of the Great Exhibition the previous year, to use art to educate the wider public and to inspire designers and manufactures.
Collection database: http://collections.vam.ac.uk [accessed 19 September 2016].

Wellcome Collection
83 Euston Road, London NW1 2BE
+44 (0)20 7611 2222, info@wellcomecollection.org
www.wellcomecollection.org
The pharmacist, philanthropist and collector Sir Henry Wellcome's collection of over a million objects formed the foundation of this collection and library, which has objects charting the history of medicine through the ages, and now has a particular interest in connections between medicine, life and art.
Collection database: www.wellcomelibrary.org/search-the-catalogues/ [accessed 6 November 2016]

JOURNALS SPECIALISING IN MATERIAL CULTURE RESEARCH

H-Net Material Culture (resources, discussions, blogs and links): http://networks.h-net.org/h-material-culture [accessed 19 September 2016].

Journal of the History of Collections: www.jhc.oxfordjournals.org [accessed 19 September 2016].

Journal of Material Culture, (primarily publishes anthropological studies): http://mcu.sagepub.com [accessed 19 September 2016].

Material Culture Review: http://culture.cbu.ca/mcr [accessed 19 September 2016].

Representations: www.representations.org/about [accessed 5 November 2016]

West 86th: www.journals.uchicago.edu/journals/wes/about [accessed 19 September 2016].

Winterthur Portfolio (a journal of American material culture): www.journals.uchicago.edu/journals/wp/about [accessed 19 September 2016].

INDEX

Note: page numbers in *italic* refer to figures.

absence 4, 12, 58–9, 71, 86–91, 96,
    146
accession
    numbers xi, 44, 99–103, 107, 133,
        134, 144–5, 149, 150
    register 101, 102, 105, 134
acquisition ix, 99, 103, 107, 108, 113
    policy 98, 106
Actor Network Theory (ANT) 20,
    59
agency *see* object, agency
anthropology 6, 15, 17–19, 20, 21,
    23–4, 27, 32, 34–5, 36n.2, 45,
    49, 58
antiquarian xi, 21, 34
antiquarianism 34
Appadurai, Arjun 23–4
archaeology 4, 6, 11, 15, 16, 20,
    21–2, 33, 39n.48, 45, 55, 65,
    96–7, 117, 127, 128, 130
architecture 9, 10, 25, 65, 79, 111
archives 28, 29, 31, 96, 114, 116,
    147, 149, 155
    museum/gallery *see* museum(s),
        archives; galleries (art),
        archives
art history 6, 11, 15, 20, 25–7, 34,
    45, 49–51, 55, 105, 122
article *see* journal article
Attfield, Judy 33

Banks, (Sir) Joseph 49–52, *50*, 106
Batchelor, Ray 122, 124

Benedict, Ruth 23
Berenson, Bernard 26
blogpost 141, 151–2, 157
Boas, Franz 23, 39n.45
book chapter 153–6
Bourdieu, Pierre 20
British Empire Exhibition
    (1924–25) 61, 83, 101
British Museum 5, 7, 21, 52, 53,
    59–61, 99–102, 104, 106,
    139n.11
Brown, Bill 33

cabinets of curiosity 17, 34,
    90
capitalism xi, 17
captions 45, 142, 144–5
cast *see* sculpture, cast(s)
catalogue (of collection) 97–9, 100,
    102–4, 107, 112–13, 117, 133,
    143, 149
    card 103–5
    entry 98, 101, 132, 134, 137,
        149
    online 12, 97, 99, 100, 103–7,
        108, 110, 112, 129, 137
categorisation 22, 24, 35, 55, 67n.6,
    76, 99–100
    see also classification
ceramics 4, 9, 25, 74–5, 128, 149,
    150
    Jingdezhen 31, 55
    porcelain xiv, 46, 53–5, 64,

74, 100, 107, 123, 132–3, 150
chopines 135–7, *135*, *136*
Clarke, Grahame 21
classical (era) 9, 25, 56, 65–6
classical (style) xii, 9, 26, 49
classification xii, 22, 35, 79
 see also categorisation
classmark xii, 44, 116
Cold War (era) 30
collecting 4, 11, 16, 28, 56, 117
 colonial 23, 34–5
 history of 11, 34–5, 52, 56–7, 65, 86, 89, 98, 100–2, 108
collector(s) 53, 56, 58, 79, 98, 104, 106, 109, 110, 113, 134–5
colonialism xii, 23, 34–5, 36n.2, 58, 59–61, 85–6, 118
commodity/ies xii, 16–7, 23–4, 72, 75, 83–5, 89–90, 122
connoisseurship xii, 26, 34, 65, 79
conservation xii, 28, 107, 118, 133–4, 139n.11, 140n.14
consumption 1, 23–4, 32, 33, 36n.9, 38n.32, 44, 74, 76–8, 84–6, 115–16
context 5, 9, 20, 24, 27–8, 32–4, 55, 56–7, 61, 79–80, 85, 89–91, 98, 103, 108, 115, 116, 121, 133–4, 137–8
Crystal Palace *see* Great Exhibition (1851)
cultural history 30, 32, 51
curator(s) 12, 16, 20, 26, 28–9, 46, 55, 59, 98, 101, 108–9, 110, 111–12, 123, 137, 152, 153, 160
curatorship 15, 20, 28–9, 71, 102, 109, 111

Darwin, Charles, 21, 23
Daston, Lorraine 1, 20
database (online) *see* catalogue, online
Deetz, James 8
department stores 114–15

design history 6, 33
digital imaging 130–1
dissertation 43, 46, 47, 141, 142, 145–6, 148, 153
documentation *see* museum(s), documentation
Douglas, Mary 23
drawing (action) 127–8, 143
drawing (object) 34, 49, 79, 99, 102, 105, 106, 107, 123, 144

English literature *see* literary studies
engraving xiii, 49, 51, 118
ephemera xiii, 31, 45
ethics *see* research, ethics
ethnography xiii, 18, 20, 23, 36n.2, 39n.45
exhibition(s) 43, 80, 85–6, 113, 114, 117, 143, 148
 catalogue entry 156–7
 catalogue essay 156
 labels 148–51
 online 141, 148, 151
 reviews 152–3

feminism 27
fetishism 17
Finley, Gregg 122, 124
First World War 18, 44, 84
folklore 29
Franks, Augustus Wollaston 101–2
furniture 20, 106, 107, 111

galleries (art) 12, 66, 95, 98, 105, 106–7, 114, 156
 archives 107–8
Garrod, Dorothy 21
gender 1, 30, 48, 63, 80, 82, 83–5, 87–8
Gerritsen, Anne 31, 46, 73–5
global history 27, 34, 41n.65, 59, 74–5, 89–90
gift(s) 18–19, 23, 35, 51, 53, 56, 102, 160

glass 25, 132
Grand Tour 34, 65
Great Exhibition (1851) 65, 86

Harman, Graham 19
Hegel, G. W. F. 25–6
Heidegger, Martin 19, 20, 33
Henare, Amiria 8
heritage sites 6, 7, 11, 12, 86, 95, 97,
    110, 111–13, 158
historical geography 33–4, 46
historic houses *see* heritage sites
history of art *see* art history
history of science 31, 33, 34, 49,
    105
history of technology 30, 31, 74
'History of the World in 100
    Objects' project 5
hospitals 114–15, 118
human relationships *see* social
    relations
Hurcombe, Linda 8

iconography xiii, 26, 27, 121
identity 20, 32, 48, 52, 53, 64, 71,
    81–2, 84–5, 88
Imperator, Ferrante *16*
imperial history 35, 49, 51–2
Imperial War Museum 45
indigenous communities 11, 18, 23,
    29–30, 35, 39n.45, 56, 118
intangible heritage 10
interdisciplinarity 3, 15, 34, 39n.48,
    68n.12, 73, 160
International Council of Museums
    (ICOM) 102
inventory xiv, 45, 54, 62, 87, 89–90,
    93n.33, 111–12, 115–16
    probate 115
Isherwood, Baron 23

journal article 146, 153–6

knowledge production 20, 34, 35,
    52

Kouwenhoven, John 31
Kopytoff, Igor, 24

labels *see* exhibition(s), labels
Latour, Bruno 20, 59
literary studies 6, 12, 15, 32–3, 46
local history 157

McClung Fleming, E. 122, 124
macro-history 58, 76
Malinowski, Bronislaw 18–19, 36n.2
Mantegna, Andrea 53–4, *54*
Marx, Karl 17
    influence of 23, 26
material culture
    definitions 7–10
    history of field 2, 5, 6–7, 8, 11,
        15–36
    location *see* sources, location
Mauss, Marcel 18–19
Mead, Margaret 23
metal 4, 123, 131
    silver 78–80
metalwork 25
methodology xiv, 10, 15, 24, 44–8,
    57, 66, 70–92, 97, 113, 117,
    143, 145–7, 159
methods 12, 21, 22, 26, 32, 70–3, 76,
    138, 146–7
    comparative 27, 46, 52, 58, 72,
        105, 124, 135–8, 144, 147
    qualitative xv, 51, 72–3, 76, 92n.2,
        152
    quantitative xv, 72–3, 76
Metropolitan Museum of Art
    135–6
mezzotint xiv, 49
micro-history 57–8
microscopy xiv, 12, 125–7
Miller, Daniel 24
Morelli, Giovanni 26
museum(s)
    archives 107–8, 117
    audiences 5, 6, 15, 29, 98, 161
    catalogues *see* catalogue

documentation xii, 28–9, 38n.40,
    96, 98–106
donors 98, 100, 101, 103, 108,
    150
education 28
history of 23, 65, 98, 107
labels *see* exhibition(s), labels
roles and priorities 5–6, 28–9,
    38n.40, 98, 102, 110, 118
visiting *see* research, visits
Museum of English Rural Life
    (Reading) 45

National Maritime Museum
    (London) 45, 63–4, 99, 105
National Portrait Gallery (London)
    106
National Trust 111
Natural History Museum (London)
    105
Naval Exhibition (1891) 64
Nelson, (Lord) Horatio 63–4, *63*
network(s) 1, 18, 20, 34, 58–9, 106,
    159, 161

object
    agency xi, 19–20, 33, 40n.60,
        83–5
    analysis 121–40
    biography 22, 24, 53, 56, 57, 58,
        74–5, 102, 132–4, 143, 149
    handling 109, 113, 118, 122–5,
        130
Ogoga of Ekiti, Ikere 60–1, *60*
Olowe of Ise 60–1
oral history 30, 70, 114
Owens, Alistair 33

painting (action) 25, 52
painting (object) 9, 27, 34, 45, 49,
    51, 53–5, 62, 106–7, 111, 123
patina xiv, 131
patronage xiv, 27, 51
Panofsky, Erwin 26
Pearce, Susan 7, 8

peer review 151, 154
Pennsylvania Dutch Folklore Center
    29
Petrie, William Flinders 21, 22
photogrammetry xiv, 130
photograph 45, 107, 116–18
    albums 9, 10, 85, 117
    equipment 129
    for publishing 113, 141–3, 155–6
    in writing-up 141–2, 147
    see also sources, visual
photography 12, 117
    of objects 102, 125, 127–30, 156
Pitt-Rivers, Augustus 8
Pitt Rivers Museum 59
plastazote xiv, 123
porcelain *see* ceramics, porcelain
portraits 9, 49–52, 79, 106, 117, 147
positivism xiv, 26
post-colonial theory 27
primary sources *see* sources
prints 9, 49, 99, 106, 123, 144
private collections 38n.40, 113–14,
    118
probate inventory *see* inventory,
    probate
production 1, 17, 20, 22, 24, 32–3,
    38n.32, 46, 48, 55, 56, 64, 79,
    103, 116, 117, 132
provenance xv, 28, 34, 38, 97, 102,
    103, 109, 112, 114, 115, 116,
    124
Prown, Jules 25, 121–2
public history 140, 157, 159–61
publication
    acknowledgement 11, 143, 156
    permissions and copyright
        113–14, 129, 142–3, 144, 156
    references 144
    see also photography, for
        publishing

race 48, 58
radiocarbon dating 21
radiography 127

reception xv, 27, 54, 65–6
recording information 44, 72, 96–7, 105, 113–14, 125–31
references *see* publication, references
registration numbers *see* accession, numbers
Relational Museum 59
relic(s) 63–4
religion 35, 62
   institutions 27, 62
   objects 27, 58, 62
   practice 62–3
Renaissance xv, 9, 54, 62–3, 65
research
   ethics 95, 113, 115, 118
   outcomes *see* blogpost; book chapter; dissertation; journal article; exhibition(s), labels; exhibition(s), reviews
   planning 10, 11, 43–69, 72, 96, 97, 109–10, 112, 118
   questions 12, 15, 43–4, 46–67, 72–3, 82, 96, 98, 112, 113, 138, 146–7
   schedule 66
   visits 95–7, 108–12, 114, 125, 129
restoration xv, 134, 140n.14
Richmond, Vivienne 80–2, *82*, 128
Riello, Giorgio 32, 40n.50, 46, 73
Royal Collection (London) 99
Royal Society 51
Rumohr, Karl Friedrich von 26

scale (of research project) 57–8, 147
Scharf, George 106
Schlereth, Thomas 8
Science Museum (Manchester) 7
sculpture xvi, 25, 34, 59–61, 65–6, 106, 132
   cast(s) xi, 65–6
secondary literature 44, 45, 47, 66, 84, 110–12, 137, 155
Second World War 2, 21, 29

Senos, Nuno 89–90
Sequence Dating System 21, 22
sexuality 83–5
silver *see* metal, silver
social history 7, 26, 29, 32, 49
social relations 1, 18, 20, 24, 59, 91
social science 2, 20, 24, 37n.19, 146
Society of Antiquaries 21, 37n.14
sources
   location 7, 28, 44–6, 57, 66, 70, 91, 95–120
   selection 70, 72
   textual 7, 31, 44–6, 54, 58, 75, 79, 82, 86, 91, 115–18, 138
   visual 9, 25–7, 44–6, 75, 80, 86, 115–17
South Kensington Museum *see* Victoria & Albert Museum
spectrometer xvi, 127
spoliation xvi, 102
Stallybrass, Peter 33
Styles, John 75–8
survival (of material) 4, 15, 28–9, 31, 45, 55–6, 58, 61–2, 71, 82, 86–7, 98, 108, 116

textiles 4, 77, 81–2, 88
Thatcher Ulrich, Laurel 57–8
thesis *see* dissertation
'thing theory' 33
three-dimensional (3-D) scanning *see* digital imaging
Tilley, Christopher 70
'tool analysis' 19
Trentmann, Frank 32
Turkle, Sherry 1

value 1, 4, 8, 9, 17, 18, 53–7, 67n.3, 72, 75, 79, 89, 111, 113
values 1, 4, 38n.35, 53, 84, 118
Vasari, Giorgio 25–6
Victoria & Albert Museum (V&A) 65, 129

Warburg, Aby 26
websites
  museum 95, 108, 110,
    143
  see also blogposts
West, Benjamin 49–52, *50*
Wheeler, Sir Mortimer 21

Winterthur Museum, Delaware 30
  Winterthur Portfolio 30
women's history 29, 30, 32, 82
Wunderkammer *16*, 17
  see also cabinets of curiosity

Zanzibar Exhibition (1905) 85–6